C000176515

Philosophy Through Storytelling

Pauline Purcell

Speechmark Publishing Ltd
70 Alston Drive, Bradwell Abbey, Milton Keynes MK13 9HG,
United Kingdom

www.speechmark.net

Published by **Speechmark Publishing Ltd,** 70 Alston Drive, Bradwell Abbey, Milton Keynes MK13 9HG, United Kingdom

Tel: +44 (0) 1908 326 944 Fax: +44 (0) 1908 326 960

www.speechmark.net

002-5666 / Printed in England by CMP/4020

British Library Cataloguing in Publication Data
A catalogue record for this book is available from the British Library

ISBN 978 0 863887727

Contents

Introduction 4

The Guidance 5

What can philosophy do for your groups? 6

A framework for running sessions 7

How to get started 7

A typical session outline 7

Step-by-step guide 8

   1 Pre-session games 8
   2 Setting the rules 9
   3 Question warm-up 10
   4 Main stimulus introduction 12
   5 Main question generation 13
   6 Selection of questions for main enquiry 13
   7 Main enquiry 14
   8 Last thoughts 14
   9 Session evaluation 15
  10 Wind-down 15

A few 'matters arising' 15

The Stories 17

   1 The New Puppy 18
   2 The Toy 20
   3 Zoya's Surprise 22
   4 Polly's Shoes 24
   5 The Little Rosebush 27
   6 Brer Rabbit 31
   7 The Salt Seller and his Donkey 36
   8 Jacob and Esau 39
   9 Into the Woods 43
  10 Chanticleer 48
  11 Sir Perceval 52
  12 The Judgement of Paris 57
  13 King Solomon 62
  14 Lady Godiva 66
  15 Calandrino's Pig 71
  16 Orpheus and Eurydice 76
  17 Rescue in the Southern Ocean 80
  18 Miracle Landing 84
  19 The Real Robinson Crusoe 89
  20 Marco Polo 93
  21 Socrates 98

Introduction

Welcome to Philosophy Through Storytelling.

Perhaps you are wondering what philosophy can do for your groups.

Perhaps you have decided to try a few sessions and would welcome some support.

Perhaps you have attended a Philosophy for Children (P4C) training course, know that it is something you want to implement but would appreciate a hand to hold while you find your feet.

Well, the news is good: this book is what you need!

This book contains detailed guidance and a set of short stories, with notes, for use in the sessions.

There are companion question cards and picture cards, available from this publisher, which would be of value in developing your skills in P4C. It is to these cards that referral is made in the guidance notes, although you can, of course, derive questions and images from other sources.

New groups may struggle with the framing of philosophical questions and the companion sets are designed to help with building your community skills in this area. Briefly, it is helpful to have a set of question cards to hand. These may be used as 'warm up" short questions for the whole group, or offered as a range from which to select the main question for discussion in depth. They provide a way into philosophy that should build confidence in handling questions, and hopefully, inspire communities to build collections of questions themselves, using different formats eg. 'Which is best,...or...?' The picture cards are useful on whole, or small group basis, in provoking participants to start creating their own questions from a stimulus, and to begin to discover through practice, which questions provide the best basis for philosophical enquiry.

Philosophy for Children (P4C) training courses

It is well worth attending a course to help with the methodology described in this book, and the organising body in the UK is SAPERE. Contact them on **www.sapere.org.uk** to find training to suit you. The Level 1 course usually lasts for two days, is really enjoyable, and will give you some grounding and confidence. Practitioners who are not in schools will very probably find the course suitable too. Please discuss your needs at the time of booking.

I cannot teach anybody anything;
I can only make them think
(Socrates)

The Guidance

What can philosophy do for your groups?

Socrates is quoted as saying 'An unexamined life is not worth living'. Time for reflection on our lives is a healthy option that all too often is crowded out by the pace and noise of modern life. Whether you are working with school pupils, students or adults, philosophy offers the opportunity to develop thinking skills that have both personal and academic application. And, contrary to popular belief, you do not need to be super-intelligent, or living in an ivory tower, to do it!

Here are some comments that I have heard when working with philosophy 'first timers':

I feel I know the people in my group much better.

I realise that I must respect what the others say. It's much more worth listening to than I expected.

It makes your brain hurt!

We don't normally get chance to talk like this.

We can disagree with each other without having a row.

I would like to apologise to everyone for messing about at the beginning. This is worth doing.

It is great to hear what others think/believe.

I need to raise the quality of questioning with my class; they are capable of so much more than I realised.

We see a different side [of some of you] to what we normally see.

Some parents complained that their children were no longer satisfied with one word answers.

I didn't know they could think like this.

A framework for running sessions

In a philosophy session, which is usually about an hour long, the group (or 'community of enquiry') will go through a 'warming up' process, examine a key stimulus, generate a question or questions from that stimulus, agree to focus on one question and share, challenge and develop views on that question. Finally, they will consider how well the process went, down-tune and end the session. Just as it is the group that will determine the focus, it is also the group that will set the rules for the conduct of the group and determine the level of success achieved. It is the normal procedure that participants will sit in a circle and that nobody dominates the process.

As leader, you will facilitate the process, initially providing support and direction, aiming all the while to grow a self-managing, self-perpetuating group with shared leadership.

This methodology was developed for use in schools, but is equally valid, with allowances made for age and place, in the community centre or the pub, and can be used with all ages from five to 95.

Setting up the space

P4C is done in a circle, and chairs are best for anyone over about eight years old. If you do sit on the floor, then everyone, adults included, should do so if they are able to. I avoid the situation where anyone sits outside the circle and so I expect classroom assistants to join in with the session if they are there. It is not helpful for any other activity to be going on in the room because this detracts from the sense of 'something important going on' that develops in sessions that flow well.

You need pencils or pens and paper; a flipchart placed as part of the circle is very useful. You will probably need some kind of talking token for passing hand to hand, for the 'one person talking at a time' convention; this can be a soft ball, a small soft toy such (very popular even at secondary level!), or I often use a lavender 'bean bag' when we will be throwing across the circle. Also useful are counters or pre-cut squares of paper for voting, but there is more on the tokens issue below.

A typical session outline

1 Pre-session game

2 Setting the rules

3 Question warm up

4 Main Stimulus Introduced

5 Main Question generation

6 Selection of question for main enquiry

7 Main enquiry

8 Last thoughts

9 Session Evaluation

10 Wind-down

I have not suggested timings, because they will vary according to the experience and needs of the group. You will find that the time spent on the early stages will decrease as experience grows, leaving more time to be spent on the main enquiry. Indeed, with a new group, you may find it best to have a few split sessions, generating the questions in one session, and selecting and pursuing the main focus in a second. Very small children, and possibly participants with learning difficulties, will not manage anything like an hour and should perhaps have their philosophy sessions in chunks of about 10 minutes spread out over the day.

Step-by-step guide

1 Pre-session games

The aim of this pre-session activity is to get everyone relaxed, focused and in a good mood before getting down to the serious business of the session. What you choose to do will depend on thecircumstances. A lively group will need a quieter activity following break time, for example, while a less confident group might need a very lively game to help the members to forget their self-consciousness and pull together. Below are some of the games I use.

The name game

This apparently simple activity is much harder than it appears and provokes laughter and concentration. It is also really useful for establishing who is who if you are not too sure!

Participants stand in a circle; person A says the name of another participant, B, and walks to where B is standing. B must name C and leave that space before A arrives to occupy the space vacated by B. Similarly, C must name D and must have moved before B arrives, and so on in a chain reaction. Failure to move before being touched on the shoulder by the advancing person eliminates the player named, who must sit down, allowing the player who eliminated them to choose again. The key point is that players must *not* move their feet before saying a name, otherwise they are 'out' and the previous player takes up the thread of the game.

The leader needs to call when players are 'out' and be really strict, this makes the game more fun.

The alien

This game is sci-fi inspired. The rationale is that Earth has been invaded by telepathic controlling aliens. Only one human, 'the investigator', is immune to the control and must save the world by detecting the alien. Participants stand in a circle and a chosen 'investigator' must leave the room while the group chooses an 'alien' who will control the group's movements.

The investigator is called back in to stand in the centre of the circle. The alien makes small movements copied by the rest of the group. The investigator has three guesses as to who is doing the controlling.

Guardian

You will need a chair in the centre of the circle, a blindfold, something to protect, such as a small box or a coin, and a 'weapon' such as a lightly rolled sheet of paper – I sometimes use a length of foam pipe insulator.

The blindfolded guardian sits on the chair with the 'treasure' at their feet and brandishes the 'weapon'. You point to a player who will then attempt to creep up and steal the treasure before being touched by the weapon – and thereby suffering instant death! Successful thieves in turn become the guardian. Keeping the rest of the group really quiet adds to the fun and focus.

Zip, zap, bong!

Think of 'Chinese whispers' or a Mexican wave to get an understanding of this useful focus and concentration game. Players pass an action round the circle on a 'receive it and pass it on' basis. There are three possible 'messages' : 'zip' is spoken accompanied by a right hand, palm down, small horizontal sweep from left to right; this message should be picked up by the next player standing on the right. 'Zap' is spoken accompanied by a left-hand, palm down, small horizontal sweep from right to left; this message should be picked up by the next player standing on the left. 'Bong' is spoken accompanied by a gesture beginning with hands on either side of the speaker's face, palms facing and the sweeping downwards through about 90 degrees until pointing at a chosen recipient anywhere in the circle. Recipients may choose to perpetuate the message received or change it to one of the other two options.

This is a non-contact game; you may need to make that clear! As players become expert, you could set a second message chain going.

Morph ball

Players sit in the circle; a player is 'handed' an invisible ball which then changes into an object of their choice. The player mimes its shape or use while the others try to guess what it has become. The successful guesser is 'thrown' the reconstituted ball and carries out their chosen mime, and so on. This game is a good one for establishing a calming focus.

Granny's shopping

This traditional game is also good for establishing a calming focus. Player 1 says, 'I did my granny's shopping and I bought ... (names object). Player 2 repeats the sentence, including player 1's item, and adds a second. Player 3 repeats everything so far, adding an item; and so the list grows, the group striving to keep going for as long as possible.

Count down

This is amazingly hard and helps develop still focus and group sensitivity. The aim is to count down to zero with only one person speaking a number and with no other communication allowed.
Anyone can decide to say the next number in the sequence. If two or more people say a number the count resets to 10 again. Do not be surprised if they can't do this! I move on before too much frustration sets in.

Fruit bowl

Only play this if you are confident you can control the group! It is a good game to play to warm up a diffident or shy group.

My safety rules, outlined at the start and rigidly adhered to, are:

1 no pushing *at all*

2 only one person per seat

3 no chair must be allowed to tip *at all*.

The game stops *at once* if any of the above occurs.

Players sit in the circle and you allocate a fruit name to each, going around the circle, apple, pear, peach, banana (four is sufficient).

You say the name of a fruit and everyone with that fruit name swaps seats.

You can say two fruits or three if you like as numbers diminish.

If you say 'fruit bowl', everyone moves.

Players must move if their fruit is called.

Remove a chair in each round by turning it to face outwards, and eliminate players who cannot find a chair to sit on. They can watch from the vantage point of the reversed seats. The game continues until everyone is 'out' except the last two, who become the winners.

Agree/disagree

In this game, three chairs or markers are placed across the room, preferably away from the circle. You make clear which chair stands for 'agree', 'disagree', and 'undecided'. Next, make a statement. 'Marmite is delicious' will do for a starter; participants move to stand in a group next to the appropriate chair. Progress to more sophisticated statements, perhaps 'nuclear power is always a bad thing' or 'we should ban cars'. At this stage, give players on either side of the argument a chance to argue their point and, hopefully, persuade others to join them.

2 Setting the rules

It is an important part of the group dynamic that the community itself sets the rules for each enquiry. Participants rapidly get the hang of this section and will refer back to successes and need for improvement noted from previous sessions.

I do take a lead in the early life of a group by explaining my 'respect rule'. This is that the community can only function if members feel safe to say what they wish without fear of ridicule or attack; that to disagree is fine but we can 'disagree politely'. I explain that if this rule is broken, I will stop the enquiry at once, adding that this will not involve anger or recrimination, merely that it has become plain that the group is not quite ready to work in this way and that we can try again another time. So far, it has never been necessary to stop.

Typically, rules that groups will decide to set include respect, careful listening, one person speaking at a time, keeping to the point, and referring to what previous speakers have said before progressing to one's own point of view.

3 Question warm up

I always explain that philosophy is all about questions; that it is about deciding what questions to ask and then exploring them. It is not necessarily about finding answers. I also make it clear that I do not have 'the answers'. This is important in that we so often look for the obvious or simple solution to questions, but it is good to look further on occasion, or to realise that sometimes there is no answer and that it is OK to hold some things in a state of uncertainty. After all, life is not always clear, and learning to deal with ambiguity is an important skill.

From the schools viewpoint, this is especially important because we run a fairly narrow curriculum in the UK with clearly defined outcomes; therefore teachers will often have a model in their head of what a 'right' answer will be like and their interactions will tend to show that bias. Pupils become expert at 'reading' the teacher and will tend to stay in the (unconsciously) 'approved' channel. In fact, at first it can be quite difficult to wean some groups off this dependence.

Philosophical questions

So, if questions are what philosophy is about, what kinds of questions do we need? Somewhat unhelpfully, the answer is 'philosophical questions'. That is to say, questions that are sufficiently rich in possibilities for discussion. In working with groups, you might approach this issue by talking about 'dry' and 'juicy' questions. 'If you were thirsty and had a choice of only a cream cracker or a nice juicy apple, which would you choose?' Then illustrate this concept by asking a group member their name. The group is invited to reflect on how much thinking was required to answer this question. Obviously, the answer is 'not much', and so this is exemplified as a 'dry' question. Then ask the same person what they are planning to do about global warming, and insist on some detail in the answer if need be. This will usually produce a pause for thought, which is a sure 'tell' that more thought is required – a 'juicy' question, in fact.

Framing philosophical questions is a skill in which the group will need practice, so question warm-up will take up a lot of time in the early stages of a group's development, but it is time well spent because the benefit will be evident in later enquiries.

Some suggested activities

It is possible to start with question cards, with questions such as 'What if we could never say "no"?' You will readily think of, for example. 'Should we always tell the exact truth?'; 'What makes a holiday a holiday? These questions need not take too long at this point; they are intended to get 'thinking' exercised and ready to go. You can always return to promising questions as a main stimulus at another time.

A useful source of questions is *The Little Book of Thunks: 260 Questions to Make Your Brain Go 'Ouch!'* by Ian Gilbert, Published by Crown House. ISBN 10-1845900626.

One easily made resource, which I have used a lot, is to have a set of A4 sheets of coloured paper. Lay them out on the floor in the circle, asking, for the first few, what colour the paper is. This is obvious, so again exemplifies, 'dry' questions. Having laid them out, you can now proceed to the kinds of questions that the group can begin to see as 'philosophical' 'juicy'. Ask: 'Which is the most exciting/sad/angry/bossy/boring/selfish colour?' Then ask for reasons why these choices were made. In order to avoid copycat answers, you can give each person a counter or voting token, and ask them on a count of three to place their token on the colour of their choice. Then those who chose a particular colour can be asked to go and stand by the coloured paper. They can then be asked why they chose it; the reasons can be listened to and other members of the group can be asked to join them if the reasons were good enough for them to have changed their mind.

It is worth highlighting the possibility of changing one's mind on hearing persuasive reasoning as being an important factor in the philosophical method. For some participants this is a release from the habit of adopting and doggedly sticking to a viewpoint, and so is well worth incorporating at an early stage.

Question creation

Your group members need to become adept at creating their own philosophical questions and this is the next phase in development. Your first session may not get beyond this point, in fact, but that is fine for now. In later sessions this section will probably fall out of use as the group gains skill in formulating questions and can progress to the main stimulus at once.

Pictures are a very useful way of working through this part of the session, a selection of suitable picture cards is available in the companion picture pack. As with the coloured papers, you can lay out a selection of pictures in the middle of the circle for participants to look at. It may help them to be invited to walk around them for a closer look. Next, they lay out their voting token on the picture that most engaged their interest.

This time you will send off the participants in groups of about three with pencil or pen and paper to write some 'juicy' questions related to the picture they chose. Give adequate time for drafting, and help those who may need literacy support, but do not expect spelling and neatness at this stage; ideas are more important.

Each group will read out the question it chose as being the most philosophical. You can ask the group, in a spirit of positive peer assessment, to decide whether the question can be and, if so, how. You should find that this collaboration really helps move the questioning forward. It is important that questions generated are treated respectfully, even if not used on a particular occasion. 'Left over' questions could be stored in a notebook, to form a group question bank, to which members of the group are able to refer for ideas for future enquiry.

4 Main stimulus introduction

The main stimulus is intended to generate a set of philosophical questions from which the group will choose one for the main enquiry. There are any number of things you can choose as your main stimulus; news reports, artefacts, stories, pictures, poems, short biographies, seasonal events, drama, trading games: whatever is capable of producing a number of interesting questions.

This book contains stories that have been tailored to fit the needs of a philosophy session in that they are short enough to be read under tight time constraints, but offer material for thought. When you need further material, there are many published assembly books which should be in most schools; and Robert Fisher's acclaimed 'For Thinking' series, published by Nash Pollock, will provide many more.

The pictures in the companion pack have been chosen as offering enough to furnish the main stimulus, used alone or sometimes paired with another image. If I need a picture on a particular topic, Google Images will usually provide it.

Artefacts are a great resource. I have used all of the following: a CBE medal, a Trafalgar medal, a WW1 German matchbox cover, a compendium of games, two boxes, one of them battered, the other 'bling', with a £5 note in one (usually the battered one), an empty shampoo bottle. You will be able to bring your own items to the table and so too will the group if they are asked to, and if trust has been well established.

You could have an enquiry based on a particular topic: Henry VIII, healthy food, Ancient Egypt... It may be helpful to have someone 'in role' or a symbolic picture or object as the focus, so that questions can be generated as 'questions we could ask Henry VIII', or 'questions we could ask a cabbage(!)', or 'questions we could ask a pharaoh or slave or tomb builder'.

In one school I know, each class, from reception upwards, keeps a large scrapbook with a big question mark on its cover. Inside are the questions generated by their philosophy sessions, and these are referred to as a stimulus for working through the topic.

5 Main question generation

Generating the main question from the stimulus can be done as described in the 'Question creation' section above. You may like to increase the range and number of questions generated by having everyone write down their choice of question individually. Or you can have the questions dictated to a scribe at the flipchart or have groups send up one member to write theirs. It's an operational choice, largely dictated by time and age or ability constraints. It is a good idea for the participants to add their names to the questions.

6 Selection of question for main enquiry

The next stage is to select one of the questions generated for the enquiry. By now you will have a number of these, either on your flipchart or in the centre of the circle. You may find it convenient to number them at this point. Some questions will bear a sufficient resemblance to others for them to be grouped together and treated as one. Participants should be asked to suggest these pairings or groups, and discussion will probably follow.

When it seems that the questions have been narrowed down as much as is practicable, it is time to choose one. It is worth reading the questions aloud to remind everyone what is on offer. Then proceed to the vote. I tend to be working on the floor at this stage with the questions laid out in the middle of the circle. It is relatively easy to give participants a couple of voting tokens or pre-cut slips of paper each for literally casting their votes. If the questions are on the flipchart, a 'thumbs up' vote can be used. It is good to vary the process to allow a bit of sophistication here. If you go for a single vote, a narrow majority will mean that most participants did not choose that question. Sometimes you can offer two votes at once, to be spent as the participants wish; alternatively, you could run the voting in two rounds, eliminating all but the top three questions before the second round.

However the process is run, you should end up with a choice acceptable to most participants. Do keep the other questions: they can be used later (see above), and it validates the effort of creating them if they are.

7 Main enquiry

We are now at the heart of all good sessions, the enquiry itself. It is useful to write up the question on the flipchart so that it is easy to see. The question writer(s) may take the opportunity to explain the thinking behind their question at this point. An examination of the question's wording is useful, allowing key words to be identified and shades of meaning explored. You can then pass a 'talking token' round for first thoughts. It is *always* all right to 'pass': often there will be a member of the group who is largely silent, possibly for several enquiries. This does not matter; they will be reflecting and thinking, which is sufficient and when they do contribute, it will probably have been worth waiting for. In fact P4C suits shyer people and often help them to blossom.

Now is the time for a free exchange of views. When someone wishes to speak, they can hold out an open palm, showing they have something to offer. The talking token can be gently thrown by one speaker to the next. As the group matures, this formality will be less necessary, speakers becoming more attuned to each other.

Developing the dialogue

At first, it is likely that participants will want to make their point, possibly without reference to other contributors. You will need to move them on from this position and encourage active listening. One way of doing this is to 'chain' the conversation. Each person must begin by referring to the previous speaker by name and mentioning something they have said before agreeing, disagreeing (with reasons), or going on to make a separate point. It is relatively easy to achieve this significant improvement with a bit of persistence on your part.

Just because there is an expectation of respect and trust in your community of enquiry, it does not mean that disagreements cannot be expressed and explored: far from it! Remember that 'disagreeing politely' is a handy maxim. Participants can be asked to provide examples of what they mean, sweeping statements can be challenged, focus maintained, counter arguments and examples advanced. Essentially, it is the argument that is under scrutiny, not the person who is advancing it. Research indicates that, given encouragement and guidance, the quality of discourse improves over time.

From time to time, it may be helpful to appoint group members as observers, who will watch the enquiry, and report back to the group on how well they are doing in developing an agreed aspect of the work, such as listening, challenging assumptions, and advancing examples and counter-examples on either side of an argument. Thus the group consciously takes responsibility for its own development.

8 Last thoughts

When the time allocated for the discussion has elapsed, or when you judge that the discussion has ended spontaneously, you can begin drawing the session to a close. Go round the group members again for their brief final thoughts: a sentence is all you need. It may become clear that the group would like to return to the discussion, in which case you could do so, after a brief warm-up, in the next session. If the discussion ended early, don't worry, but just proceed with last thoughts.

9 Session evaluation

This section is an opportunity to evaluate how well the session went; how well participants felt that the rules set at the beginning were adhered to; how listening skills were improved; how well points were made; and how well the group retained the focus of the discussion. Targets may be set for the next session if that is what the group wishes to do.

10 Wind-down

You may not need to do a wind-down, but if the session has been emotionally demanding, it is a good idea to bring everyone back to earth with a repeat of the starter game or one which you know the group likes to play.

A few 'matters arising'

Early sessions will need compromise on content and timings. You cannot hope to step straight into smooth session outlines; being patient and building skills will pay off.

As mentioned earlier, it is always OK to 'pass' in P4C. Contributions made voluntarily will be all the better for being unforced.

It is best not to use 'hands up' for speaking because the authority in P4C is not with the group leader, but with the group. I think the open hand symbolises something to offer, which is nice. Thumbs-up (or down or sideways) voting can be done close to the chest and may be easier for shyer participants in signalling their opinions.

'Leftover questions' can be a valuable resource for further thinking. The scrapbooks mentioned earlier are an example of good practice in this respect. You may also like to consider having a home or school philosophy book in which each question is given its own page. Group members can assume responsibility for the book in turn, taking it home for family members to add their thoughts on the topic.

It is fair to say that philosophy excites interest in many families, and as the group grows in confidence, it might be an enjoyable experience to invite them to a philosophy tea party. Refreshments and an enquiry demonstration would be the order of the day.

Some participants may find a session disturbing, because the topic touches sensitive areas for them. You will need to exercise judgement here and be prepared to do some follow-up pastoral support if necessary. If someone is plainly unhappy at the group's choice of focus at the outset, I think it fair to make it quietly possible for them to leave the room for the last sections, but offer support afterwards if needed. This has only happened once in my experience, and it was with an adult group.

Summary

- Philosophy is accessible to people of most ages and ability; and it can be life enhancing.

- Sessions are flexible, but ideally follow a regular pattern of activity.

- The optimum number of participants is 20.

- Circle seating is best.

- The session was examined in detail with suggestions of what might be done:

    1 Pre-session game – to set people at ease, and help them focus together.

    2 Setting the rules – the group disciplines itself and learns to become more effective together.

    3 Question warm-up – philosophical thinking is a question-based skill that improves with practice.

    4 Main stimulus introduction – the provision of a focus for the group enquiry and a number of ways in which this may be done.

    5 Main question generation – opportunity to create philosophical questions arising from the main stimulus.

    6 Selection of question for main enquiry – a democratic process whereby the group decides on what is worthy of further discussion.

    7 Main enquiry – the heart of the session, a chance to explore a question in some depth, and how to improve the dialogue.

    8 Last thoughts – opportunity to draw the threads of the discussion to a close.

    9 Session Evaluation – the group evaluates its level of skill and progress, possibly setting operational targets for the next session.

    10 Wind-down – moving back from a level of possible intensity of engagement into the everyday and ordinary.

- Building group skills and working towards slicker sessions will take some time, patience and sensitivity, there are no shortcuts.

The Stories

These stories are intended to provide your group with a starting point for an enquiry. They are therefore brief enough to be read in a very short time, and for participants to be able to scan the text for question opportunities within the context of a P4C session. Most are retold or recast from familiar sources, with a bias in the narrative towards raising unanswered questions.

In using the stories, it would be good to have the chosen story projected on to a whiteboard in the room, or for enough copies to be printed off for there to be one between three participants. The suggested questions at the end of each story should not be displayed or circulated; they are a fall-back option for prompting a struggling group to produce its own line of questioning.

The stories have been arranged in approximate order of age appeal and comprehension difficulty, beginning with material that is very simple in content and moving to the more complex. Group leaders should not be bound in any way by this arrangement, but should make a choice according to their own judgement of what will engage their group. The real differentiation arises from the kinds of questions that the group is able to derive from the material used.

1 The New Puppy

Lee and Jordan were twins. It was their fifth birthday, and to their delight, Grandma and Grandad gave them a puppy. The puppy was a wriggly, round black and white baby sheepdog. They named him Ben.

'Take good care of Ben', said Grandad, 'make sure he has plenty of water to drink, and feed him every morning and every evening.'

'And remember that he is only a baby', added Grandma, 'he needs lots of sleep and gentleness. He will be more fun when he grows a bit bigger.'

'Yes, Grandad, yes Grandma,' replied the twins, 'we will take good care of him.'

At first, Lee helped Mum to feed Ben every morning and Jordan helped every evening. If Ben was sleepy, they left him alone to let him rest, and if he wanted to play, they played gentle games. Everything was going well.

Then Jordan stopped helping Mum feed the puppy. 'I'll come in a minute,' Jordan would say, but stayed watching TV instead.

When the puppy was sleepy, Lee let him rest, but Jordan would sometimes tease him and try to make him play, which made the puppy a bit snappy.

At playtime, Lee was still gentle with the puppy, but Jordan sometimes got too rough with Ben, which frightened the little dog.

One day, Lee and Jordan came in from doing the grocery shopping with Dad. Ben ran to meet Lee wagging his little tail. Jordan called Ben to come to him but the puppy stayed where he was.

'Dad,' asked Jordan sadly, 'why does Ben love Lee more than me?'

1 The New Puppy   Source: Original

There are themes here of kindness, unselfishness, consistency, love, trust and responsibility.

- What should Jordan do now, and why?

- What if Mummy had made Jordan come to help feed Ben?

- How will Lee feel about this situation and what should Lee do?

- Are Lee and Jordan boys or girls or one of each?
  Explore your reasons for what you decide.

- Were Grandma and Grandad right to give Ben to the twins?
  Why, or why not?

2 The Toy

Tom bought a new toy. He came back from town with his grown-up sister holding the big bright box very carefully.

Tom had never bought anything himself before, but he had saved up carefully until he had enough money for this special toy.

Tom knew that the toy was very special because he had seen it on the TV. In the adverts, it could fly all by itself and its owners felt like heroes, you could tell from the looks of excitement on the faces of the children on the screen.

The box looked great too, with pictures of the shining wonderful toy, doing the most amazing things. Tom could hardly wait to get it home and open it. In fact his sister had to stop him opening it on the bus.

When they got home, Tom sat down on the living room floor with his treasure and began to undo the sticky tape holding the box closed. Mum came in from the kitchen to watch.

At last the box was opening, Tom's heart beat fast, soon he would be just like those happy boys and girls on TV.

What was this? The box contained several lumpy pieces of grey plastic which looked nothing like the pictures on the cover of the box, and some sheets of brightly coloured stickers. Tom's heart stopped dancing and sank down into his shoes instead.

'Mum, there's been a mistake,' he said.

2 The Toy   Source: Original

This story carries themes of expectation, perseverance, trust, influence, disappointment, dream versus reality, and advertising standards.

- What if Tom had been given the money rather than saving up for the toy?

- Do outside appearances always tell the truth?

- How should Mum try to help Tom now?

- Can we trust what we see on TV?

- Should toy manufacturers be allowed to sell unfinished toys?

3 Zoya's Surprise

Zoya loved surprises. If Zoya had a present wrapped in shiny paper and tied with ribbon, she was very happy and opened her parcel as quickly as she could.

For a while, each new game or toy made her happy, but then their newness wore off. She got used to them and even a bit bored. 'Daddy,' she said, 'why do my presents not keep me interested forever?', but Daddy only listened and smiled kindly. 'Mummy,' said Zoya, 'why do my presents not keep me interested forever?', but Mummy only listened and smiled kindly too.

That night, when Zoya was asleep, Mummy and Daddy made a telephone call to Grandma in Pakistan. Zoya knew nothing about it.

A few weeks later, the postman brought a parcel. It had come all the way from Pakistan and it was addressed to Zoya.

Excitedly, Zoya tore off the brown paper, expecting to see shiny wrapping paper underneath; but there was only another layer of brown paper. Puzzled, Zoya opened this brown paper too. Inside was a battered old biscuit tin, bent and a bit rusty; but there was a bright, white label on the lid, written in Urdu.

'What does it say, Daddy?' asked Zoya.

'It says, "Ask Mummy" teased Daddy, who was watching TV.

'No, it doesn't,' laughed Zoya, 'tell me.'

Daddy picked up the box, it rattled a bit as though something hard was inside. 'The label says "Take good care of what you see inside and life will always be interesting".'

Mummy came in from the bedroom, holding the baby. She said, 'This parcel is not really a surprise to me, it is something I had when I was a little girl. Granny sent it because we asked her to, and I know that the whole family must open it together.'

So, with all the family looking over her shoulder, Zoya opened the battered tin box. Inside was a beautiful, polished metal mirror, with a richly decorated frame. Reflected in the centre were four smiling faces, looking into the mirror.

3 Zoya's Surprise Source: Original

This is an opportunity to think about values, family values in particular, about the transience of interest in new things, and about the attraction of the unknown.

- What if there were never any surprises?

- Why do we get bored? What does being bored mean?

- Why would Zoya's family be more interesting than a new toy?

- How can people stay interesting?

- Did the fact that Mummy once owned the mirror make the present nicer? Why, or why not ?

4 Polly's Shoes

Polly had some new shoes; they were black, shiny, patent leather with ankle straps and she loved them. Polly wanted to wear them at once to walk home, but Mum and the shop assistant agreed that they might get scratched and put them carefully in their box for her to carry, while Polly wore the brown lace-up shoes in which she had come shopping. Polly was three and too young to go to school, but she called her lace-up shoes her school shoes so as to be more like her big brother, who was five and did go to school.

When they got home, Polly had her old coat put on so that she could go and play in the garden. 'I think I will wear my new shoes,' she said.

'Oh no,' said Mum at once, 'we are keeping them for best. You must wear your school shoes to play in the garden.'

Polly was really angry that she was not allowed to wear her new shoes. She went up the garden, to carry on digging a hole to Australia with the old garden trowel, but she was in a very bad temper indeed.

While she was digging, Polly had an idea. If her old shoes were lost, she would have to wear the new ones, wouldn't she? She pulled off her brown shoes and tried burying them in the hole, but she thought they would be too easy to find. She tried hiding them in the hedge, but they were too easy to see.

The house next door had been empty for a very long time, and her brother had told her there were ghosts in it; so Polly's next idea seemed to her to be very daring. She crept through a hole in the hedge and buried the shoes in the garden of the empty house. It was quite frightening and it also turned out to be much harder getting back than she expected.

Polly went inside to Mum wearing only her socks. 'I shall have to wear my new shoes after all,' she announced, 'I've lost my school shoes.'

After that, nothing went the way she had planned. Mum and Grandma took Polly back up the garden and tried to make her tell them where the shoes had gone, but she would not. Then Polly had to stay in the house, while she watched Mum and Grandma searching the garden for the lost shoes.

'Just you wait until your father gets home,' said Mum, when she and Grandma gave up looking for the shoes. It was not the happy afternoon Polly had planned.

Dad was not pleased at all when he got home from work and heard what had happened. Polly was in big trouble from everyone now, so she decided to tell them what had happened to the shoes.

'I buried them next door,' she admitted to Dad.

'Nonsense,' said Mum, 'she can't reach the gate'.

'I crawled through the hedge' explained Polly and showed them the place. Much to her dismay, nobody believed that she could have crawled through the hedge there and, looking at the tiny hole, Polly, too, wondered how she had managed.

'Come with me,' ordered Dad, and he took Polly through the gate and into the empty house's garden. 'Show me where you buried them.'

The garden looked completely different when you came through the gate, and Polly was so muddled that she could not find the place where she buried the shoes. Dad was really cross with her, and tried to make her show him the place, but she could not remember at all.

'The shoes are not there, Polly is a liar,' announced Dad when they returned home.

In the days that followed, Polly did creep back into the garden a few more times but never could find the shoes.

In deep disgrace with everyone, Polly was taken back to the shoe shop, a few days later, to buy some more shoes for everyday wear. Even the shop assistant looked displeased with her. Polly was miserable, especially since everyone now thought she was a liar.

Many years later, a new neighbour found the shoes when digging his garden. 'So you did bury them next door,' said Mum and laughed.

4 Polly's Shoes Source: Original

The story deals with truthfulness, authority, consequences
and anger.

- Should Polly have been allowed her own way over the shoes?

- Polly was three years old, so did she understand what she was doing?

- Why did the garden look different when Polly went through the gate?

- Was Dad right to call Polly a liar?

- Do you think the finding of the shoes made any difference?

5 The Little Rosebush

Once upon a time there was a little rosebush. She lived in a lovely garden, and was the loveliest thing in that garden. Her rosy stems supported glossy green leaves and delicate tiny thorns of deepest red. Her flowers were her crowning glory, being purest white with hearts and tips of palest gold. At night, in the moonlight, these flowers shone like silver, and by day, in sunlight, their hearts glowed like golden fire.

The Little Rosebush had many admirers, who gained pleasure just from seeing her, day by day. In fact the only inhabitant of the garden who seemed uninterested in the Little Rosebush was a Busy Brown Hen, who seemed wholly taken up with the business of feeding her family.

One sleepy afternoon, a white butterfly visited the Rosebush and laid one white egg on a leaf before fluttering away. Nobody noticed, nobody at all.

So it was that three weeks later, a green caterpillar hatched in the night and began munching steadily at the Little Rosebush's leaves. It ate and ate. The Little Rosebush was horrified; she tried to shake off the green caterpillar, but it hung on tightly and ate and ate. In sorrow, the Little Rosebush hung her head, her flowers and leaves drooped, and she shivered although there was no breeze.

Dawn came and up rose the Sun. He climbed higher and higher in the sky and then looked down, expecting to see the Little Rosebush in all her beauty. Instead, there she was, drooping and sorrowful. The Sun sent a sunbeam, dancing and glittering down, to ask what was the matter.

'Oh!' cried the Little Rosebush, 'there is a caterpillar eating my leaves, and soon I will be eaten away unless somebody does something about it.'

'Oh dear!' cried the sunbeam, and dashed back to tell the Sun what had happened.

'Oh dear!' cried the Sun, 'in that case I am not going to shine any more until somebody does something about it,' and with that he hid behind a big black cloud.

When evening came, the Moon rose gracefully and was surprised to see the Sun sulking behind a big black cloud. 'What is the matter?' she enquired.

'There is a caterpillar eating the leaves of the Little Rosebush, and soon she will be eaten away, so I am not going to shine any more until somebody does something about it.'

'Oh dear!' cried the Moon, 'in that case, I am not going to shed my silver light until somebody does something about it,' and she hid behind the big black cloud too.

Pretty soon it was time for the Nightingale to leave her nest and sing her song in the silver moonlight; but there was none. She flew up towards the big black cloud. 'What is the matter?' she enquired.

'There is a caterpillar eating the leaves of the Little Rosebush, and soon she will be eaten away; so the Sun is not going to shine any more, and I am not going to shed my silver light until somebody does something about it.'

'Oh dear!' cried the Nightingale, 'in that case, I am not going to sing any more until somebody does something about it,' and she flew down to her nest and put her head under her wing.

The Nightingale's nest was just above the Little Rosebush, in the branches of a vast Oak Tree. Now the Oak Tree realised that the Nightingale was not singing the nightly song that he enjoyed so much. 'What is the matter?' he enquired.

'There is a caterpillar eating the leaves of the Little Rosebush, and soon she will be eaten away; so the Sun is not going to shine any more, and the Moon is not going to shed her silver light; and I am not going to sing any more until somebody does something about it.'

'Oh dear!' cried the Oak Tree, 'in that case, I am not going to drop any more acorns until somebody does something about it,' and he did not.

Soon it was breakfast time and a frisky little Squirrel woke up in his drey, high in the Oak Tree. The Squirrel scampered down to the ground to look for acorns, but there were none to be had. Of course he had buried lots of acorns, to eat later, but he could never remember where he had dug the holes. The Squirrel looked up at the Oak Tree. 'What is the matter?' he enquired.

'There is a caterpillar eating the leaves of the Little Rosebush, and soon she will be eaten away; so the Sun is not going to shine any more, and the Moon is not going to shed her silver light; the Nightingale is not going to sing any more, and I am not going to drop any more acorns until somebody does something about it,' said the Oak Tree.

'Oh dear!' cried the Squirrel, 'in that case, I am not going to dig any more holes until somebody does something about it,' and he scampered back to his nest, high in the tree.

Very soon afterwards, along came the Busy Brown Hen with her brood of chicks. She was looking for nice juicy worms for their breakfast, and always arrived at the same time each day because the Squirrel usually dug up lots of worms when he buried his acorns. The Hen was very surprised to find that there were no holes and no worms. 'What is the matter?' she enquired.

'There is a caterpillar eating the leaves of the Little Rosebush, and soon she will be eaten away, so the Sun is not going to shine any more, and the Moon is not going to shed her silver light, the Nightingale is not going to sing any more, the Oak Tree is not going to drop any more acorns, and I am not going to dig any more holes until somebody does something about it,' said the Squirrel.

'I see!' exclaimed the Hen, and strutted over to the Little Rosebush. In two seconds she had found and gobbled up the caterpillar. 'Very nice,' she remarked. 'Now let me give you all a piece of my mind. You, Sun, could have sent a sunbeam to burn the caterpillar and make it fall to the ground. You, Moon, could have sent the Nightingale to help the Little Rosebush, and you, Nightingale, could have gobbled up the caterpillar just as easily as I did. Oak Tree, you are near enough to drop acorns and knock the caterpillar off its leaf, and you, Squirrel, with your clever paws, could have easily picked the caterpillar off the bush. But no, you all sat around and sulked and waited for a busy person to come along and solve the problem. You should all be ashamed of yourselves.'

With that, she gathered up her chicks and went in search of breakfast, leaving behind a much happier Little Rosebush and some very embarrassed friends.

5 The Little Rosebush
Source: From a French fairytale

The story invites us to consider individual choice and responsibility, and the tendency to 'go along with the herd'. There are echoes here of the saying 'If you need something done, ask a busy person.'

- Why should the caterpillar not eat some of the Rosebush's leaves?

- Was the Little Rosebush making a fuss about nothing?

- Why do we spread stories?

- Would you say that the Hen was friendly? Why, or why not?

- This story could not have really happened, so what is its point?

6 Brer Rabbit

Brer Fox was mighty sick of Brer Rabbit. Brer Rabbit always made him look a fool, and Brer Fox didn't like it, not one bit. By rights, Brer Rabbit should have been fox dinner years ago, but, no matter how hard he tried, Brer Fox just couldn't catch this clever rabbit; and the longer he tried, it seemed, the harder it got.

There was the time, one morning in the snow, when he nearly caught Brer Rabbit, but Brer Rabbit had laid himself right in the snow and rolled like a ball away down the hill, picking up snow as he went like a giant snowball. Brer Fox had been really happy to see that ball rolling away with Brer Rabbit inside. Trapped rabbit, he was, in Brer Fox's opinion, so all Brer Fox needed to do was stroll away down that hill and dig dinner out of the ball at the bottom by the pond.

Brer Fox set off down that hill with a light heart and a swing in his step, thinking of how he had got Brer Rabbit at last and of just how he would cook him; but that was his undoing. He missed his footing and fell, rolling over and over down the hill, gathering himself inside his own giant snowball. When he got to the bottom of the hill, his snowball skidded and slithered out on to the ice and came to a halt in the middle of the pond. Could he get out of his snowball? No, he could not! There he lay curled snugly in his snow prison and wondered what to do about it.

Pretty soon he heard a familiar voice calling to him from outside his snowball. It was Brer Rabbit, of course, and he was laughing fit to burst.

'Yoh! Brer Fox, what are you going to do now? You are so stuck!'

'I'm fine,' replied Brer Fox through chattering teeth, 'I like it in here. I shall get out the same way you did when I'm ready to.'

'No way!' laughed Brer Rabbit, 'I steered my snowball to hit the tree at the bottom, so that it broke to pieces and let me out. You are in the middle of the pond, Brer Fox, on the thin ice. I can't see how you will get out.'

Brer Fox, he said nothing, nothing at all; he was too angry and too cold.

'Never mind, Brer Fox,' Brer Rabbit went on, 'the sun's up and warm, soon the snow will melt and you will get loose. Of course the ice might go first, so you will be in for a cold bath bobbing about in there. You might even sink like a stone,' he added, 'and drown. That would be too bad. Got to dash, bye.'

Now all this time, Brer Rabbit had been gently pushing that old snowball without Brer Fox noticing, he was so mad; and when he said 'bye', it had just touched the bank at the edge of the pond where the water was not deep at all, as Brer Fox found out when, much later, his snowball melted and let him go.

It was the same every time, Brer Rabbit made Brer Fox look a fool, every time.

All the other animals knew how hard Brer Fox was trying to catch Brer Rabbit and were laughing at him behind his back. He had heard the squirrels sniggering at him from the branches that time when he was about to catch Brer Rabbit, who had been sleeping in the shade at the mouth of his burrow under the tree. That time Brer Rabbit had woken suddenly and cried out that there was a giant acorn falling from the tree above, and that had made him look up just when he was about to pounce. Brer Fox had heard Brer Rabbit's laugh echoing back at him from the burrow and had got so mad he had even bitten his own tail in annoyance.

Brer Bear always asked him how his rabbit stew was cooking, and Brer Bear was bigger than he was so Brer Fox just had to grin like he was enjoying the joke, which he certainly was not; and if Brer Bear knew it all the creatures knew it... Oh yes, Brer Fox was building up a powerful hunger for that rabbit stew. He was going to show everyone that he could fix that rabbit and freeze the laughter on their furry faces.

One fine day, Brer Fox was making his way along the road when he found a barrel that had fallen from the back of a trailer and broken open in the road. Out of it oozed black, shiny, sticky tar, and all at once Brer Fox knew exactly what he would do with it. At last he had found a way to catch Brer Rabbit for sure.

Very quickly, Brer Fox set to work, for Brer Rabbit could be coming along the road at any time. He fashioned the tar into the shape of a little person, a tar baby, and propped it against the barrel as though it might be resting there in the shade. He pressed two shiny stones in for eyes and a row of acorns for a mouth. Well satisfied with his tar baby, Brer Fox hid behind a tree and waited for Brer Rabbit to come lolloping along the road, which he very soon did.

Brer Rabbit saw the tar baby and stopped mid-lollop. 'Good afternoon,' he said.

The tar baby said nothing at all.

'I said, "good afternoon",' repeated Brer Rabbit.

The tar baby said nothing at all.

Brer Rabbit was not pleased at all. 'I said, "GOOD AFTERNOON", you know,' he said again, raising his voice.

The tar baby said nothing at all.

'OK,' said Brer Rabbit, 'you are getting a punch on the nose, for just sitting, staring at me when I was being civil.' And Brer Rabbit gave the tar baby a big punch on the nose with his right paw. Wham! Squelch! Much to his surprise, it stuck fast in the tar. 'LET GO OF MY PAW!' shouted Brer Rabbit, 'I'll hit you again,' he warned.

The tar baby said nothing at all.

Wham! Squelch! Brer Rabbit hit the tar baby with his left paw. It stuck fast in the tar too. 'I'll kick you if you don't look out!' threatened Brer Rabbit.

The tar baby said nothing at all.

Wham! Squelch! Brer Rabbit kicked the tar baby with his left foot. It stuck fast in the tar. Wham! Squelch! Brer Rabbit kicked the tar baby with his right foot. It stuck fast, and he was really stuck.

Out came Brer Fox from behind the tree, licking his lips.

'Something smells good,' he remarked. 'Oh look, it's Brer Rabbit just waiting for me to pick him up and cook him for dinner. Now, what shall I do to him first? Shall I pop him into a boiling cooking pot?'

'Oh please, Brer Fox,' replied Brer Rabbit in a frightened voice, 'pop me in the pot if you like, but please don't throw me in that bramble patch over there.'

'Hum!' said Brer Fox, 'maybe I'll just skin you and roast you in the oven.'

'Oh please, Brer Fox,' replied Brer Rabbit in a more frightened voice, 'roast me in the oven if you like, but please don't throw me in that bramble patch.'

'Hum!' said Brer Fox, 'maybe I'll just frizzle your fur and fry you in the pan.'

'Oh please, Brer Fox,' replied Brer Rabbit in an even more frightened voice, 'frizzle my fur and fry me if you like, but please don't throw me in that bramble patch.'

Now Brer Fox was thinking about all the times Brer Rabbit had tricked him and done things to him that he did not like at all; it seemed to him that he should get his revenge on Brer Rabbit. All of the horrible things he threatened had had no effect at all, but there was Brer Rabbit quaking and shaking and begging not to be thrown in the bramble patch. Well that was it then, that was exactly what he would do, throw Brer Rabbit, tar baby and all, into the brambles.

He lifted Brer Rabbit and the tar baby high and with a huge effort, flung them into the middle of the thick, thorny bramble patch.

'Ow!' screamed Brer Rabbit, secretly smiling and scraping one foot free on the sharp thorny brambles. Outside, Brer Fox smiled.

'Ow! Ow! Ow!' he repeated, as he freed his other foot and front paws.

Outside, Brer Fox smiled and prepared to pick up his dinner.

After a while, all was a bit quiet. Brer Fox pushed his nose into the bramble patch. 'Ow!' he yelped, pulling it out and holding it with both paws. 'My nose!' he complained.

In the distance from far down the lane he heard a laugh. 'Stick some tar on it!' cried Brer Rabbit as he lolloped away.

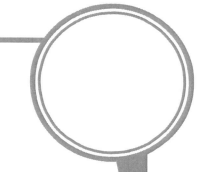

6 Brer Rabbit
Source: Traditional African/American; Uncle Remus; some original

Aspects of this story are well known and deal with trickery, but considerations of bullying, revenge and cruelty also run through the narrative.

- What if the characters were people rather than animals?

- Why is Brer Fox so mean to Brer Rabbit?

- Does acting nasty make a person nasty themselves?

- Is Brer Rabbit right to be nasty to Brer Fox? Why, or why not?

- Were the other animals bullying Brer Fox?

7 The Salt Seller and His Donkey

Once upon a time, there was a man called Sam who made his living by selling salt, that most useful of commodities. Sam owned some shallow tanks near the seashore which he would fill with seawater and leave for the hot baking sun to do its work. Over a few days, the water in the tanks would evaporate, leaving behind a layer of shining white salt, crisp and perfect as snow on a mountain side. Each week he would go to the coast with his donkey, Dina, to collect the salt that had dried. Sam would pack the salt into the two wicker baskets that hung on each side if Dina's small saddle; then together they would return to the city where the salt was needed to keep food fresh and Sam would be able to sell it for a good price.

Sam was a kind man and took great care of Dina. She had the best food to eat that he could afford to buy for her; she had a comfortable stable, cool in summer and warm in winter; her harness was carefully made and regularly checked to make sure that there were no rough patches to cause her discomfort; and last of all, Sam never asked too much of her. If her panniers were full of salt, Sam would always walk beside her, refusing to add his own weight to that of the salt.

With such a kind master, you would think that Dina would be a happy and grateful donkey, but, alas, she was not. Dina, you should know, was a very arrogant little soul; she took every one of Sam's kindnesses for granted as though they were her right. Furthermore, she was convinced that the carrying of salt was too lowly a task to be performed by a princess among donkeys such as herself.

One day, Sam and Dina were returning home with their salt, panniers full, when a small accident occurred that was to make a big difference. Dina, in crossing a small, fast-flowing river, missed her footing on the slippery rocks and fell into the water. Now Dina was never in any danger: she was a good swimmer, and Sam made it his first care to rescue his much-loved donkey. However, when they came to the river bank, Sam found that the water had dissolved all of the precious salt, and that the panniers were empty. There was no point yet in returning to the shore for more, because the sun would need all the days in the week to evaporate the seawater from the next batch of salt.

With empty panniers, Sam and Dina returned home. That week they made no money. Sam went a bit hungry, but made sure that Dina had her full amount of food as usual. In her stable, Dina thought about what had happened and an idea formed in her brain.

The next week, panniers full, Dina deliberately slipped on the rocky riverbed, dissolving the salt and coming out with light, empty baskets, with which Sam was obliged to return home for a second week. Dina was exceptionally pleased with herself and trotted home light-heartedly. Sam, however, was not pleased at all; he had seen the look in Dina's beautiful brown eyes and detected a note of satisfaction there. The more he thought about the matter, the more sure he was that Dina had not slipped by accident.

That week, Dina went without her favourite foods and had to make do with boring, ordinary hay instead, which did not please her at all. Sam was even less well fed, and as the week passed, he devoted a lot of time to considering what he should do to make Dina well behaved again.

At last it was time to return to the shore. Dina haughtily paid no attention as Sam loaded the baskets, then they began their usual homeward journey. Dina did just wonder why her panniers felt a bit lighter than usual, but came to the conclusion that Sam had decided to fill them less full in the hope that she would cross the river more securely. Well, she thought smugly, he would soon realise that, light or heavy, those panniers were going to get a ducking.

They came to the river crossing, 'Take care, Dina,' warned Sam. Dina snorted in derision and once more allowed herself to slip, panniers flooding with water.

It was at this point that Dina realised that something had gone wrong. Instead of becoming lighter, the panniers were heavier; so much heavier that she needed all her strength, and Sam's assistance, to struggle up the bank out of the water. As she stood trembling on the bank, water ran from the baskets and trickled down her sides. The panniers were the heaviest they had ever been.

'Come along, Dina,' called Sam, taking her leading reins, 'we must hurry to get these sponges to market. What a shame that the dipping in the river has filled the sponges with water and made them twice as heavy, but there is nothing I can do about it. I am sure they will fetch me a fine price. I may even buy myself a stronger donkey, for if you keep falling over, I shall have to sell you, my dear.'

Dina was a very tired and very thoughtful donkey when she returned to her stable that night; but she had learned her lesson. Of course, Sam had no desire to sell his much-loved donkey, and Dina began to appreciate her kind master more. Never again did she seek to dissolve her burden of salt, and Sam prospered in business, selling both salt and dry, light sponges in the town.

7 The Salt Seller and His Donkey
Source: Aesop's Fables

The story invites us to consider fair and unfair behaviour, animal welfare, wisdom, and consequences of actions.

- Did Sam spoil Dina?

- Was Dina clever to try to get rid of the salt?

- Was it fair to make Dina carry a load?

- Should we make animals work?

- How wise was Sam?

8 Jacob and Esau

It is sad but true to say that brothers and sisters do not always get on together, even when they are twins. It is also sad but true to say that some wrong-headed parents favour one of their children over another. Such favouritism does not create happy families, and this story is about one such unhappy family.

Isaac, son of Abraham, was about 60 years old when our story begins, and in recent years his eyesight had been failing badly, to the point where he had become very nearly blind. He and his wife Rebecca had twin sons, Esau and Jacob. In addition, Isaac's old father, Abraham, lived with the family.

When Rebecca was pregnant with the twins, she was having a most uncomfortable time because the babies were always violently kicking inside her, and never more so than when she was passing a temple or another place of worship. She became sufficiently worried that she asked for advice from a wise counsellor and in answer she was given a prophecy. The prophecy was that the two children fighting in her womb would go on fighting all their lives, and that each of them would become the leader of a nation. Rebecca kept this prophecy to herself, but she always remembered it.

When the babies were born, it was Esau who appeared first. He was strong and muscular and had lots of hair, like a much older person. Jacob came into the world a very close second; in fact he was born hanging grimly on to Esau's heel as though he would not let his brother win the race to be the firstborn, and therefore their father's heir.

As the two boys grew to manhood, the differences between them became more and more evident. Esau was thickset and muscular with an impressive mane of rough hair that also grew over his chest, back and shoulders; he delighted in hunting and tracking and fishing. He loved eating and drinking and having a good time, and rarely took any interest in serious subjects. He had no interest at all in the God of his grandfather Abraham, whom Isaac and Rebecca also worshipped. Esau was his father's favourite son.

Jacob was slender and smooth skinned. His interest lay in farming and husbandry: he worked to improve his father's flocks of sheep and goats and oversaw the growing of wheat, vegetables and other crops; he was home-loving and quiet in his relaxation time. Jacob shared the beliefs of his family and, despite the many forms of religion about his home, stayed true to the worship of the God of his grandfather.

At last, old Abraham died and was buried with honour as befitted a great man. Isaac was sad at the loss of his father and spent much time alone grieving. Rebecca and Jacob were mostly at home and did what they could for Isaac. Esau went hunting as usual. One day Jacob prepared a traditional lentil stew for his father and was just getting ready to serve it when Esau arrived home, hot, dusty and very hungry.

'What's that you've got?' he demanded.

'Lentil stew,' replied Jacob, 'but I didn't make it for you, so back off.'

Esau was really very hungry and, because he was used to getting his own way with his weaker brother, and was thoughtless as well, he felt that the stew was his by right and he was going to get it. 'Hand it over, or you'll regret it,' he said, raising his fist.

'Not likely,' responded Jacob, 'I'd rather pour it on the ground than give it to you,' and he seemed about to tip the stew away as he spoke.

'No, wait, I'll pay you,' replied Esau. 'Name your price,' he added rashly.

'Oh, well,' said Jacob airily, 'I could let you have it in exchange for allowing me to be father's heir.'

'Done!' exclaimed Esau, 'Now give me the stew, Shorty.'

'Promise?' asked Jacob, holding on to the stew,

'Yes, I promise,' snapped Esau and grabbed the pot.

As Esau gobbled the stew down, he had just one uneasy moment when he wondered if he had made a mistake, but since he was not given to thinking, and had no intention of keeping his word, he was easily able to forget the whole episode. Jacob, however, did not.

Seven years passed and Isaac lay dying. He told Esau that he was feeling that his time was near and had decided to confirm his heir in his inheritance by giving his blessing, formally and irrevocably, to his son. By this, of course, Isaac meant that he would give his blessing to Esau, and would do so as soon as Esau returned from a special hunting trip with the meat that his father wanted to eat, as a last treat cooked by his favourite son. Rebecca overheard the conversation and felt that there was no time to lose if Jacob was to claim his promised inheritance.

Rebecca called Jacob and told him to obey her instructions exactly. He was to bring in a goat from the herd, slaughter and skin it, bringing her the hide and the meat. All this he did. Rebecca then made the meat into a delicious stew using Esau's own highly spiced recipe, one he often did for his father. When the stew was ready she made Jacob cover his head and shoulders with the rough-haired goatskin and carry the food in to his blind father. He obeyed.

Isaac was surprised that his son had returned so quickly with the promised food, and asked the supposed Esau how he had managed to be back so soon. And Jacob replied that God had helped him, which was a mistake on Jacob's part because Esau never, ever talked about God. Isaac, thinking that he should make quite sure that it was indeed Esau that was offering him food, called Jacob nearer so that he could feel his skin. This Jacob did, and feeling the rough, hairy goatskin made Isaac a bit more certain that it really was Esau. Finally, and to make sure, Isaac asked, 'Are you my son and heir Esau?' and Jacob, meaning that he was indeed Isaac's son and heir, answered that he was. Finally convinced, Isaac ate and drank and then gave his blessing, making Jacob the inheritor of all that he possessed and senior to Esau, his brother.

It was at this moment that Esau returned, carrying the game his father had requested. When he understood what had happened, he flew into a rage and demanded that Isaac should withdraw the blessing he had given to Jacob. Regretfully, Isaac explained that it was out of his power to do such a thing, since the blessing came from God and was his to give only once.

Esau, realising that Isaac felt he had no choice in the matter, swore most dreadfully that on the day of Isaac's death, Jacob, too, would be a dead man. Rebecca, knowing of Esau's desire for revenge, then persuaded Isaac to allow Jacob to go away from home, to live with her brother Laban until it should be safe for him to return. So Jacob went, and there became the victim of a deception himself; but that is another story.

8 Jacob and Esau   Source: The Bible

Family jealousy, having favourites, consequences of lying and the importance of promises all have echoes in this episode from the Old Testament.

- Is it always bad to compete?

- Were Isaac and Rebecca good parents? Give reasons.

- Was Esau a bully or just a big brother?

- Was Jacob right to hold Esau to his promise?

- Are there any 'goodies' in this story? Who are they? What is good about them? Check each character carefully.

9 Into the Woods

Hi! Oh! You are SO not going to believe what happened to me. Let me tell you about it.

Well, you know my stepmom grounded me for going into the woods on my own? Yeah. Well I wasn't going to put up with that, not from her, anyway; Daddy wouldn't have grounded me for such a little thing so why should she, I'd like to know? I do wish Daddy hadn't decided that we would like to spend a few weeks at our backwoods home and then get called to LA on business. Just her and me, yuck!

So, I decided I would show her. I set my cell phone alarm for really early next morning, got dressed. What? Oh, yeah, in my Burberry jacket, Ralph Lauren jeans and a Stella McCartney T-shirt, I just wore my old Gucci sneakers 'cos I was not going to ruin my new ones in the woods, and I took my new blue Dolce and Gabbana bag, though now I wish I hadn't done that. Oh yes, I was going back, to the woods, on my own, so she would know not to mess with me.

Well, I let myself out of the house and ran off down the drive as fast as my legs would take me. This was fun. I thought about how my stepmom would go wild as soon as she knew I was missing. She'd probably blame the help for letting me go, but that didn't matter, I had made sure nobody saw me.

It was sort of OK, walking under the giant trees, birds twittering and all that kind of stuff. I decided to go as far away from HER as I possibly could, to make sure that she'd have a real bad time finding me. Well, I walked for a good long time and then I thought I'd take a break, maybe see if I could get a signal on my cell phone so's I could tell you what I was doing.

I sat down under a tree and opened my Dolce and Gabbana blue bag. Ohmigod I had only left my cell phone in my bathroom. Disaster! Well, it was no good going on without my cell phone, 'cos (a,) I couldn't ignore her calls when she tried to contact me and (b,) well, I guessed I might have needed it if I got lost or something. I got right up and went back the way I had come. Or so I thought, anyway.

Pretty soon I realized that I had no clue as to where I might be, which was kind of worrying, I suppose. Yeah, you could say I was kind of worried. I walked on, feeling a bit thirsty and hungry and stuff until I came upon a trail running through the woods.

Come on! I thought, this looks good, I'll follow the trail 'cos it's gotta be going someplace, after all.

I followed the trail and pretty soon it came out at this little log cabin, kind of cute it was with a flower patch and a swing in the porch, but really small. I went right up and knocked on the door, 'cos I felt sure that whoever lived there would be glad to help me, especially when they knew who I was, or rather who Daddy is. Nobody came to the door so I knocked again, and then sat down on the porch swing to wait for somebody to turn up.

After a while, oh at least five minutes, I got fed up with waiting and decided that 'whoever' would not mind if I used their landline to call a cab or something. So I walked right in. No landline, whoever heard of people having no phone in the house? Looking around some, I could tell that really poor people lived here, I mean, no designer furniture or kitchen appliances at all. There were some pretty retro-chic bowls on the table that would have been worth a few dollars in the right sales outlet, but nothing much else. I noticed that these bowls had some breakfast food in them. Now I normally have only fresh orange juice and strawberries for breakfast, but after my early walk this stuff smelled good enough to eat. There was no one about despite breakfast being laid for three, so I decided to try just a bit of the large bowl's contents. OK, it was porridge, but yuck was it salty! The next had soo much sugar in it that clearly somebody had no respect for their waistline, but the third was just fine, and what do you know? I ate it all before I realised! Oh well.

These guys were so poor that their furniture looked all homemade and even the cushions did not match, but I decided to sit inside for a while, I was feeling a bit tired after my early start. The first chair left me with my feet dangling way off the floor, no way.
The second chair was so soft I sank right into it so it felt like my chin was hitting my knees. No good either. I really liked the third chair, it was a bit small but really comfortable so I let myself relax. Ow! Next thing you know, I'm on the floor and the chair is a wreck; worse, my Ralph Lauren jeans have come off badly with a huge tear at least an inch long on the waistband. I am now really upset and decide that Daddy should sue these hicks for having dangerous furniture in their homes.

There was no place else to sit in the kitchen so I decided to look for the den – there might be a TV and DVDs to watch while I wait for help to arrive, I think. Imagine! There was no den, no lounge, no anything; just that tiny kitchen and a bedroom out back. There were three beds in there so I guessed everyone had to share in this house. It's really dumb to be poor I think.

The first bed looked ok but turned out to be lumpy as hell, so I tried the next. This was real soft, but the feather pillows were bad for my allergy, so I moved on to the little bed in the corner. That was not bad, not bad at all. Next moment, I was sound asleep.

I really do not know how long I was there, but something woke me. The next thing I knew I was looking at these three ugly hairy faces. 'Have they never heard of *waxing*?' I wondered, like one of those mad things that goes through your head when you're in a dream. Next minute, I am wide awake and screaming like I am gonna die. I tell you, I was out of that cabin and out along the trail so fast!

I ran about a mile before I realised I had left my precious Dolce and Gabbana bag on the porch. I really, nearly cried then; but there was no way I was going back, oh no! I wandered along that trail forever, and it did not seem to be getting me anywhere. Was I fed up!

Eventually, I saw a clearing up ahead and I sat down in it to take a rest. Not long after I sat down, I thought I could hear the sound of a helicopter over the trees. I took off my Burberry and spread out wide on the ground so the checked lining would show against the grass. This was no time to worry about mud on my clothes, I thought. Then I jumped up and down and screamed like crazy, hoping they would see me. They did. The helicopter circled the clearing and eventually came in to land.

I put on my jacket and my most winning smile and approached the helicopter as it landed. It was not a nice private one like Daddy's and it was being flown by police officers. 'Oh, hi,' I said as sweetly as possible, 'would you mind terribly taking me back to town? Then I can get a call through to arrange a car to take me home.'

Well they were quite honestly the rudest men I have ever met! They checked that I was me, if you see what I mean, packed me in the back seat, strapped me in and off we all went without a word. I tried again, 'Thank you soo much for the lift, officer,' I said into the headset I found hanging by my seat.'

'This is not a lift, miss, it's a rescue. Your stepmother is frantic with worry and the rescue services are out across half the state.'

'Oh,' I said. To be honest I was a bit surprised to hear this but I tried to laugh it off, which was a mistake, I realise that now.

That officer read me such a lecture, I am sure would have cried if I had listened to even half of it. He said that he thanked heaven that I was not his daughter and lots of other stuff. Well, I nearly said that I'd be surprised if he had a daughter who looked half as good as me, but luckily I saw my reflection in the window and decided that I should wait until I had had some serious grooming attention before saying anything to anyone.

The helicopter took me down on our front lawn, and there was my stepmom looking really upset, which surprised me.

Later that day, I got a text from Daddy. He was so not pleased with me and threatened to take the cost of the rescue out of my allowance, which means I shall have to wait a whole extra month to replace my lovely handbag! Unless I can get round him, of course.

9 Into the Woods
Source: Traditional meets *Hello!* magazine!

Themes here are selfishness, stupidity, spoiling children, wealth and poverty, arrogance and moral blindness.

- Was Goldilocks well brought up?

- Which is more important, a well-groomed body or a well-groomed mind?

- Who is most to blame for Goldilocks's behaviour?

- Are fashion labels important?

- Was the police officer right to say what he thought? Why, or why not?

10 Chanticleer

Once upon a time there lived a poor widow; and yet not so poor, for she had the necessities of life and was content. She kept a smallholding in which she had a pig, a few sheep, two cows, six hens and a very fine cockerel called Chanticleer.

This Chanticleer was king of the farmyard, he was quite sure of that. Every day he strutted about, his bright red comb and wattles glowing in fine contrast to his ebony black beak, and his fine blue legs and white nails showing elegantly against the mud of the farmyard. Chanticleer took pains to stay in good voice, crowing the hours more regularly than any town clock, with extra performances for special occasions and feast days. All in all, he knew himself to be an impressive bird, worthy of his position as lord of the dunghill and hero of the hens: a very fine creature indeed.

Chanticleer kept a harem of six wives in the henhouse, but of all the six his favourite was the lovely Dame Pertelote; with her it was a case of true love, and she was Earth's bliss to him. Pertelote listened to him adoringly as he showed off his fine voice, and admired him for his reputation for bravery, a reputation Chanticleer had been very careful to create, it must be added.

Imagine Dame Pertelote's distress, therefore, when Chanticleer, sleeping beside her on his perch, awoke with a throat-wrenching squawk. 'Whatever is the matter, dear Chanticleer?' she enquired anxiously.

'Death! Doom! Destruction!' cried Chanticleer, still between sleep and waking and shaking so much that the perch trembled violently. 'Keep him away! Don't let him get me!'

'Wake up!' commanded Pertelote, 'you will disturb the others with your disgraceful display of cowardice. Awake! Be my hero!'

At length Chanticleer managed to become fully awake and regain some self-control. He was then able to tell his favourite wife what had troubled him so badly. It was a dream; and in the dream a fearsome creature had entered the farmyard in search of Chanticleer's life, no less. It was like a dog, and yet not a dog, he told her falteringly; it was reddish brown, with dark tips to its ears and a white tip to its bushy tail. Worst of all, it had a pointed narrow jaw filled with the most fearsome sharp teeth. Nobody, he declared, could have imagined a more frightful monster than had appeared in this dream. Clearly, it was a premonition of death, and there was no hope of him escaping its warning. 'It's an omen, that's what it is,' he quavered.

Dame Pertelote was not quite pleased to find her dashing hero turned to a quivering heap, and said so quite roundly. It was clear to her that the dream was a warning of quite a different kind: a warning against overeating, as – she assured Chanticleer – she had seen him doing the previous day. 'It's constipation you have got,' she told him, 'and a decent dose of laxative will set you right. A light diet of juicy worms and a nibble of some dandelion and burdock from the cabbage patch will get you going again; just stay off the corn. I cannot love a coward, you know, so pull yourself together.'

In the light of day, Chanticleer was able to forget his night terrors and was soon strutting his stuff around the farmyard, arrogant and noisy as usual. At feeding time, he headed straight for the corn and was helping himself generously when he felt a wifely eye upon him. Dame Pertelote had not forgotten the dawn disturbance even if he had, and the message in that look was quite clear: 'worms and dandelions, or else.'

Chanticleer made a great show of scratching at the ground near the feeding trough as though he had been on a worm hunt all the time, and as anyone but a silly female would have easily seen; then he strutted majestically down towards the cabbage patch at the bottom of the farmyard. He did not know that his dream was about to come true.

There was a crafty old fox, Russell, who lived in the woodlands and fields near the widow's smallholding. This fox was old in cunning and had had many a good meal at the widow's expense. He it was who had assassinated and eaten Chanticleer's respected parents, and listening morning, noon and night to Chanticleer's constant noise had developed in him a taste for cockerel flesh once more. Accordingly, the fox laid his plans: overnight he had tunnelled under the widow's fence and was now lurking in the cabbage patch, waiting for his opportunity to arise.

Chanticleer strutted between the cabbages, picking off the odd caterpillar and nibbling at dandelion leaves. His attention was taken by a butterfly that was disturbed from one of the plants, and there he saw Russell crouched low between the rows. Now, Chanticleer's first instinct was to fly to safety at once, but he thought of how impressed Dame Pertelote would be by a show of bravery, so he stood his ground and let out a faltering crow. Even to Chanticleer it sounded wavering and unimpressive.

Russell, hiding a sly smile, made his move. 'Good morning,' he said, smooth as eiderdown, 'I do hope I didn't disturb you, my dear sir. You see, I was intimately acquainted with your dear father and, remembering how wonderfully he sang, I have come to hear you. I wondered if you could produce the same wonderful volume as he did. I can see him now, eyes closed, head up and neck stretched to the heavens, singing away. Ah, that was what you might call a song,' he added, and sighed reminiscently.

Chanticleer was very keen to show this stranger that he could equal or, preferably, outdo his father in the matter of crowing and immediately assumed the position described by the fox, adding his own touch by stretching upwards so much that he was on tiptoe.

Russell seized his chance and Chanticleer's neck. He tossed Chanticleer's body on to his back, and then set off at speed towards the woods, free of pursuit and feeling pretty pleased with himself.

Meanwhile, Dame Pertelote and the ladies had been indulging in a little genteel dust bathing to get rid of the fleas. She happened to glance in the direction of the cabbage patch and saw her beloved being spirited away by the exact monster he had described in his dream. She and the other ladies set up such a cry of alarm that the widow came out to find out what the problem might be.

The widow saw the fox on the run with Chanticleer and raised the alarm, and released the dogs, Harrow and Welaway. She and her two daughters ran after the fox as well. The neighbours and their dogs joined in the chase, so that by the time Russell reached the woodland edge, there was a full-scale pack coming after him.

'I wonder,' croaked Chanticleer, 'that you, fine animal that you are, should be such a coward as to run from an old woman and a few mongrel dogs. If I were you I would show them what I think of them. I would stop here and cry out, 'I'll show you who is boss. I will eat this fine cockerel here right in front of you. Just try to stop me, that's all.'

Russell was much impressed by this speech. He wanted to prove that he was more than a match for the people and dogs of the village, and Chanticleer's suggestion went down very well. 'Just a minute, then,' he said, reducing his hold on his victim in order to speak, 'let me show them my best side.'

Chanticleer took his opportunity, broke free of the fox's slackened grip and flew up into the nearest tree.

When Russell saw that his prize was out of reach he said, 'Oh dear Chanticleer, I do hope I have not alarmed you in any way. Do please come down from the branches.'

'Oh no,' replied the cockerel, 'you will not trick me twice. I am not that stupid.'

'Oh, I wouldn't be too sure of that,' replied the fox preparing to make his escape. 'The amount of noise and dust you create in that farmyard doesn't leave you much time for using your brains, you know. I'll be back.' With that the fox disappeared into the trees, leaving Chanticleer to his rescuers, a quieter more thoughtful bird.

10 Chanticleer
Source: The Canterbury Tales

The story looks at ideas of vanity, foolishness, trickery and courage.

- Is Chanticleer living with an unreal idea of himself? If so, how?

- Is it fair to laugh at someone else's vanity?

- Was the fox wiser than Chanticleer?

- Is trickery the same as wisdom?

- This is a very old story. Can we still learn anything from it?

11 Sir Perceval

At the court of King Arthur, the Knights of the Round Table pledged themselves to protect the weak, to behave well to ladies and to use their strength for the good of all. In all these things, they promised on their life to obey their king. It was called the Oath of Chivalry.

Arthur had invented the Round Table and the Oath of Chivalry because, when he became king, England was a place where 'might was right'. In other words, the strongest could do what they wanted and literally get away with murder because they were good at fighting and bullying. Arthur wanted a change; he wanted his knights to use their power for justice and he wanted England to be a better place. He was succeeding, too. At first, the idea of not being a big bully was difficult for some of the knights to understand, but as they got used to doing the right thing, they found they liked it better than the old life and settled down happily to rescuing maidens, defeating dragons and vanquishing ogres and false knights. Almost everything at Camelot was perfect. Well, except for Sir Perceval, that is.

Sir Perceval was not the cleverest knight ever to brandish a sword, and although he had taken the oath along with the others, he was having difficulty in seeing how it meant he should be better behaved. Sad to say, if a maiden needed rescuing, it was often Sir Perceval she needed rescuing from. He was fine with smiting dragons and ogres, and even with defeating false knights up to a point, but when it came to the ladies, he was a disaster!

You could have laid the blame on Sir Perceval's old dad, I suppose. 'Treat 'em rough, son,' had been his advice when on his tenth flagon of wine; but really there was no excuse. Perceval knew that his mother had run away to join a nunnery and that his sisters had got married as early as possible, and all of them had taken the greatest of care to choose a husband who was nothing like their father at all, in any way whatsoever. Luckily, Sir Perceval was nothing like his father, really, he just didn't know it yet.

The problem came to a head when Sir Perceval decided that it was time for him to get married. He captured the first likely lady he met and carried her off to his castle. Luckily she was a clever girl and, after laying him out flat with a frying pan, made her escape not half an hour later. Putting the frying pan carefully out of sight, Sir Perceval managed to make the second lady at least stay for supper, but in capturing her, he had ruined her nice new dress and she cried about it so loudly that he decided to let her go, too. He took care not to damage the third lady he captured, and not being sure quite what do next he shut her up in a tower for three days and forgot to feed her. She might have died up there but, fortunately, two of Perceval's fellow knights saw her waving from the window and made him let her go too.

Each of these ladies in turn complained to King Arthur about Perceval's dreadful behaviour; and in great anger he sent for his knights to attend court. When everyone was assembled he made Sir Perceval stand before them all and commanded the herald to read out the list of accusations. It did not sound at all good. 'Well, what have you to say?' asked the king.

'I was doing what my father said, treating 'em rough,' replied Sir Perceval. 'I was only getting a wife for myself', he added, looking confused.

'You have broken your oath and your life is forfeit,' pronounced Arthur, sternly ignoring one or two of the pageboys who had collapsed into giggles. 'Prepare to die tomorrow. It is the law and must be obeyed.'

Then the Lady Guinevere, Arthur's beautiful queen, spoke. 'Have mercy, great king,' she said, 'this knight must learn a lesson. Pray allow him three weeks to find the answer to my quest. After that time he shall return. If he has succeeded, then spare his life. If he has failed, then he must die.'

Arthur smiled in relief, for he really did not want to put Sir Perceval to death. 'What is this quest, my lady?' he enquired.

'Sir Perceval must return with the true answer to the question, "What do women want?" or die in the attempt,' replied Guinevere.

'So be it,' declared the king, and dismissed the court.

Sir Perceval mounted his horse and rode away from Camelot, wondering how he could possibly fulfil his quest. His journey took him through town and countryside, he travelled by the seashore and far inland. Everywhere he went he asked the same question of the women he met: 'What do you really want?,' and never did he get the same answer twice. Some said they wanted gold, some jewels, and some fine clothes. Hard-worked serving women said they wanted rest, idle ladies of leisure said they wanted an occupation to relieve their boredom. Some wanted to be married; others wanted to be single again. Some wished for a baby in their arms, others wished that their children were grown and no longer needed them. The list grew and grew. It was seemingly endless, and Sir Perceval was in despair of finding a single answer.

One thing he did learn, however, and that was that his father had clearly been wrong. The women he met valued courtesy and disliked being bullied, which Perceval realised was pretty much how men liked to be treated too. From believing that women were very different beings from himself, he gradually came to a realisation that women were people too. It was a new and astonishing thought, and Perceval was pondering it as he turned back to Camelot. His time was up; he had no answer for the Lady Guinevere, and he knew that he must prepare to die.

A short distance from his journey's end, he passed though a dense forest. It was a soft summer's day and the sunlight filtered through the trees, creating a delicious green, dappled shade. Sir Percival dozed in his saddle. He was brought wide awake by entering a clearing and seeing there, dancing on the short grass, a group of beautiful young women. Reflecting that this would be his last chance to find an answer to his quest, Perceval urged his horse forward and drew near to the dance. Instantly, and as always seems to happen in stories of this kind, the women vanished and Perceval was left alone, as he thought. With a heavy heart he dismounted to give his steed rest and a chance to crop some of the grass.

Perceval headed for a twisted tree stump, intending to tie the reins to it, when to his astonishment it both moved and spoke. It was an unbelievably old, unbelievably ugly woman, dressed in tattered clothing the colour of the earth itself. Slowly she rose to her feet. 'I know what you need to know,' she said, looking him straight in the eye. 'I can save your life, Sir Knight, but you must pay a price for this knowledge, for it was costly to obtain.'

Looking into the old woman's bloodshot and watery eyes, Sir Percival came to the conclusion that he could somehow trust this odd old lady. 'What is your price?' he asked.

'A promise,' she replied, 'that you will do what I ask when we come into the king's presence.'

'I promise,' agreed Sir Percival. After all, he told himself, nothing could be worse than death.

The old woman called him with a twisted finger to come closer and whispered something in his ear. The smell of her breath was truly loathsome and he hastily took a step back. The old woman merely smiled through toothless gums and asked him to take her on his horse to Camelot, which he did.

King Arthur, Queen Guinevere and all the court assembled to hear the outcome of Sir Perceval's quest. 'Lady Guinevere,' he said, 'the thing that every woman wants is the right to choose for herself.'

Guinevere nodded wisely, and so too did all the ladies of the court and the serving maids peeping from behind the kitchen archway. 'My Lord King,' she said, 'we sent away a foolish man and have received in his place a wise one,' and she smiled, for she knew that Perceval's life was saved.

Then the old woman stepped forward, and knelt before King Arthur. 'Dread Lord,' she said, 'I claim the promise of this fair knight to do what I now ask in return for this knowledge he has here displayed. I claim his hand in marriage.'

A ripple of shock ran across the crowded court, but Sir Perceval, turning very pale, said, 'I promised, and that promise I will keep. Let the wedding be tomorrow morning.'

'So be it,' decreed King Arthur, and of her kindness the Lady Guinevere led the loathsome old lady away to her chambers where she and her ladies provided a bath and perfumes and rich clothing for the bride.

Sir Perceval did not sleep that night; he felt that his life would be a sort of nightmare, wedded to the old woman. However, he had realised that to break an oath is a wicked thing to do and was determined to go through with the marriage.

The next day, a splendid ceremony took place in the cathedral of Camelot, followed by a feast and dancing. Everyone tried to pretend that they were enjoying the day, and nobody really succeeded.

Finally, the couple were left alone together. The loathsome lady took one of Perceval's hands in hers. 'You have kept your promise, now I will offer you a choice as a reward. I can become young and beautiful again, if you like, but I will not stay faithful to you; or I will remain as you see me now and be a faithful wife. What is your choice?'

Sir Perceval thought for a moment about the entire lesson he had learned, then said, 'My lady, the choice is yours to make. It shall be as you wish.'

In that moment the lady was transformed into a young woman of radiant beauty. 'Because I have chosen for myself,' she said, 'I choose both. I shall keep my beauty, which was hidden from you until now, and I will be faithful to you all our lives long.' And she was.

11 Sir Perceval
Source: The Canterbury Tales

This version of *The Loathly Lady* focuses on the relationship between men and women, and traces the personal growth of one character. Medieval ideas are far removed from ours, of course, necessitating an off-beat treatment of parts of the story. Older participants may like to note that in *The Canterbury Tales*, Perceval is actually convicted of rape at the beginning of the story, and take that into their question formulation.

- How far are we influenced by our parents?

- Was the lady right in her answer?

- Is 'inner beauty' enough?

- Did Sir Perceval deserve a happy ending?

- What are the differences between men and women, apart from the obvious?

12 The Judgement of Paris

There was trouble on Mount Olympus, and for once, Zeus, king of the gods, was at a loss in deciding what to do about it. This is how the trouble started.

Zeus had decided to throw a big party, a massive celebration with ambrosia and nectar flowing with the wine and with food in vast quantities, a true banquet for the gods. Heavenly music played and all the invited gods and goddesses were having a wonderful time. Everyone agreed that it was the best entertainment ever had on Mount Olympus, but that was before Eris, the goddess of discord, arrived.

Eris, being the goddess of arguments and falling out, had not been invited to the party. In fact, everyone had gone to a lot of trouble to prevent her finding out about it. If ever there was someone to ruin a party, that someone was Eris. Unfortunately, Eris did know about this party; she had found out about it some time ago, could tell how hard everyone had tried to keep her out of the secret; and had time to plan something really special as revenge.

Eris took care that she should be the last to arrive and stalked in just as Zeus had proposed a toast to 'happiness and harmony'. The glasses froze at everyone's lips, as they saw Eris; uncomfortable glances were exchanged between those who had tried particularly hard to put her off the scent of the party. 'Hello everyone,' she smirked, 'isn't this nice? I have brought a party prize for somebody, and here it is. I really cannot stay any longer, I have just a tiny feeling that I was not invited!' And as she left with an irritating giggle, she flung a beautiful golden apple into the gathering.

Apollo, the sun god, stepped forward and picked up the apple. He held it high and it sparkled in the light of his shining face. The gods and goddesses gasped in admiration, and all were secretly hoping that the apple could be theirs. 'There is an inscription on it,' said Apollo, 'it says, 'for the most beautiful'.

Immediately, Aphrodite, goddess of love, stepped forward, 'Oh, that will be for me then,' she smiled enchantingly and reached for the apple.

'Not so fast, Aphrodite,' exclaimed Athena, goddess of wisdom and war, 'I think you'll find that I am the rightful winner of this prize. You may have a lovely body, but I have a beautiful body and a beautiful mind, which is more important.'

'The apple is a prize fit for a queen, ' stated Hera, wife of Zeus, queen of heaven, 'and therefore clearly mine, for I combine majesty with my beauty. Apollo, I command you to hand me the apple.'

Argument spread throughout the gathering; the party atmosphere was quite ruined, and Zeus realised that with so many powerful beings all in a state of agitation, it would not be long before he would have to start throwing thunderbolts around to keep the peace. 'Give me the apple,' he said to Apollo, 'and be quiet, everybody! That is my command.'

'Now hear my wisdom,' he declared to the waiting gods and goddesses. 'Here are three of us, each of the greatest beauty; and clearly, each in her way wholly deserves this prize. Which of us can judge the issue fairly? Not I, for to me my dear wife, Hera, must be the fairest, while to you others first one, then another of these lovely contestants would seem to deserve your vote. We immortals could easily go on forever arguing the issue round and round, which is the way to endless strife. Yet who should be the judge if not one of us?' Then Zeus threw his hands open wide and waited for suggestions.

Ares, god of war, spoke. 'I am surprised to be offering a peacemaking suggestion, but I know of a mortal prince of sound judgement and fairness; Paris is his name. It so happens that he entered his prize bull into a competition in which I myself had decided to take part, in the shape of a bull. Of course, I looked magnificent, and as soon as Paris saw me, he conceded victory even though, because he was a judge, he could have awarded his own animal the prize. Paris is the man for this job, mighty Zeus; you will find him in Phrygia: Paris, Prince of Troy.'

Zeus thought well of Ares' advice and sent Hermes, his messenger, to tell Paris to be at the sacred spring, on the slopes of Mount Ida, at noon the next day, ready to carry out an important judging task. Hermes sped away on the wings of his sandals and helmet, and the three goddesses went away to prepare for the forthcoming beauty competition.

The next day was itself beautiful! The sun shone in a clear azure sky, and far below lay the Aegean, blue and bright as a precious jewel. A soft, cooling breeze stirred the grey-green leaves of the olive trees that stood about the sacred spring and gave a pleasant shade to the slopes of Mount Ida, where Paris, Prince of Troy, waited to hear what his task might be.

Paris did not have long to wait. Hermes darted into view, carrying a sparkling golden apple, which he handed to Paris. 'You see, mortal, that it is engraved *to the most beautiful*,' said Hermes. 'You are said to be a just judge, and your task is to award the apple to the fairest of the three goddesses that you shall now meet. Do you understand what you have to do?' he concluded.

'I do, 'replied Paris.

'Then let us begin,' proclaimed Hermes; and at once three visions of loveliness came walking into view through the olive grove. The three goddesses were so attractive that Paris actually forgot to breathe for a moment or two, and all he could do was to stare, open-mouthed, as Hera, Athena and Aphrodite seated themselves gracefully beside the sparkling sacred spring.

Now, it should be explained that each of these goddesses had decided, quite privately of course, that there would be no harm in a little bit of bribery to help her case along; and each had come prepared to make an offer that she thought would make Paris decide in her favour.

Hera was the first to make her offer. She approached Paris and spoke softly in his ear; needless to say, her fellow competitors watched angrily as she made her offer. Hera, she said, was prepared to make Paris a gift of power; he could be lord and ruler of the whole of the known world if only he would award the prize to her. Paris bowed noncommittally; but Hera, confident that she had won, returned to her place with a smile.

Next to approach with an offer was Athena, who offered to Paris endless wisdom and unrivalled skill in war craft. Again Paris bowed noncommittally; but Athena, sure of her success, returned to her seat with satisfaction in her gaze.

Last came Aphrodite, who approached in a shower of flowers, headily fragrant, and accompanied by sweet music, charmed from the air. Paris felt his stern indifference begin to melt. 'Darling Paris,' breathed Aphrodite in his ear, 'what you really need is love. Love will bring you more pleasure and joy than all the power, wisdom and war craft in the wide world. Let me help you,' she continued, stroking his arm, 'If I win, I have a little present to give you; look into the spring and you shall see what it is.'

Paris followed Aphrodite to the spring and there arose from the water, as though in a beautiful sleep, the loveliest girl Paris had ever seen. 'Go on,' murmured Aphrodite, 'take her in your arms.'

'Who is she?' Paris asked.

'Helen, wife of Menelaus of Sparta, darling, but I wouldn't let a little thing like her marriage stand in the way of true love, you know. And she will love only you, dear Paris, I will see to that.'

Paris gazed at Helen and gazed again. Aphrodite was right, he thought; nothing could compare with sharing his life with this lovely creature, just now awakening and opening her shining eyes and smiling lovingly at Paris. No, he just could not resist her allure, and as she stretched out her arms towards him, he reached out to embrace her in return.

'Just a moment, darling Paris,' interposed Aphrodite, 'haven't you forgotten something?' Paris looked at her blankly. 'The apple, darling,' she said, somewhat less lovingly than before. 'I must have the apple, you know, or there will be no sweet little Helen to love.'

Of course, the apple was lying forgotten in Paris's hand. Unceremoniously he thrust it into the waiting palm of Aphrodite and without a backward glance carried the still sleepy Helen away towards Troy.

Imagine the triumph of Aphrodite and the anger of her rivals! Athena sped away to Greece to stir up the Athenians in support of Menelaus, warrior king of Sparta. But Hera was angriest of all and in her fury decreed that there would be no peace for Troy while Helen was within its walls; also that the love between Helen and Paris would be the doom of many brave warriors before her taste for revenge should be appeased.

So it was that a thousand ships sailed from Greece to lay siege to Troy, and reclaim Helen for Menelaus; but that is a story in its own right.

12 The Judgement of Paris
Source: Greek myth

Vanity, selfishness, misjudgement, bribery, and consequences of mistaken judgement all play a part in this well-known story.

- Should this story really be called 'A judgement on Paris'? Why might it be so?

- Is it right to use the kind of persuasion that the goddesses employed?

- Would we ever resort to bribery? In what circumstances would we be really tempted?

- Could Paris have chosen differently? What would have been a safe choice?

- The Greeks believed that the gods carried on their squabbles using mortals as playing pieces. Are people ever really used like that? In what circumstances?

13 King Solomon

Listen and learn from the wisest of all, King Solomon, of legendary wealth and fame.

It came about that Solomon, newly a king of Israel, slept on his couch. He had wakened and watched long into the night, reflecting on what a king he should be, and on how he should use his power and might for the good or ill of his people. At last, worn out with wondering, he fell into a deep sleep, and into the strangest dream he had ever had.

It seemed to Solomon in his dream that Jahveh, the mighty Lord God, was offering him a choice of coronation gifts. What should he choose? He could have anything: wealth, unlimited power, happiness, health; the choice was unlimited. Pondering deeply, Solomon came to his conclusion, made his choice, and offered it to God, hoping that it would be acceptable to the Almighty. Solomon chose the gift of wisdom. With wisdom he could rule fairly; with wisdom, he could avoid taking his nation into war and danger needlessly; with wisdom he could watch over and provide for the needs of his people. Solomon could not think of a gift he needed more.

Solomon's choice pleased the Lord God mightily, for it showed that the young man was worthy of the trust He was placing in him to lead the nation. Yes, Solomon should have his wish; he was to be the wisest of all kings of all the nations of the Earth; and because the Almighty approved of his choice, Solomon would be rewarded with power and legendary wealth and glory to match his wisdom. At this, Solomon awoke and saw the soft pink light of dawn spreading across the skies, a new day for a new king.

Days and weeks passed, and it became clear to all who stood about the throne that the young man was no ordinary king. He surpassed in grace and mercy, he was handsome and brave, and above all, wise. Older courtiers told the younger courtiers that never had the kingdom been ruled so well in living memory.

It was not just the courtiers who learned to be impressed by their young king.
The common people too began to know that, in the court of the king, they would be dealt with tenderly but fairly. Solomon was no fool and could tell lies from the truth better than any of his judges.

One day, Solomon's oldest and wisest councillors brought before the king a strange and troubling case; it was one which none of the judges could decide on at all. It involved two women and a baby living and a baby dead. So that you shall perceive the wisdom of Solomon, you shall hear at once the true story in this troubling case.

The two women, Agis and Nipa, shared a house so that they could share the costs and labour of looking after their two babies, who had been born at one and the same time. Sad to say, they were each very envious of the other, watching the babies to see which was the more beautiful, advanced and clever, and each preferring their own. Of the two, Agis was the loud in praise of her baby and disparagement of Nipa's; so, unsurprisingly, the competition between them meant that they were not the best of friends.

One dreadful morning, one of the mothers, Agis, awoke to find that her baby beside her had died in the night. Her grief was very great but not, sad to relate, as great as the rage that possessed her when she reflected that she no longer had the best and most perfect baby in the competition; a wicked thought indeed, but so it was. And one wicked thought led to one even more wicked, as is often the case.

It was still very early and nobody else was awake. Silently as a shadow, Agis slipped into Nipa's room. Taking care not make a sound, she substituted her lost child for Nipa's living, breathing baby and stealthily returned to her bed.

When Nipa awoke, her first care, as always was for her child. Imagine her shock and grief on beholding the infant deep in the sleep from which there would be no awakening. She cried aloud and wakened the whole neighbourhood with her grief.

Everyone came round to offer help and assistance, but there was nothing anyone could do. Nipa was lying, face down on her bed, loud in lamentation, while Agis sat near the doorway, strangely silent, cradling the stolen infant. Above the hubbub of noise and consternation a frail and familiar sound reached Nipa's ears. It was her baby's cry; she would know it anywhere and remember it all the days of her life. But how could that be possible? Her baby lay dead, surely?

Nipa looked up from her bed, her eyes followed the sound. It did not come from the silent crib but from near the doorway. Nipa's eyes met those of Agis and she knew at once what had happened. Loudly she accused Agis of the theft and, just as loudly, Agis denied it. The two women screamed and shouted at each other, tore at each other's hair and raked each other with their nails, but all to no avail.

Appalled, the neighbours separated the two women and sent for the judges to make a decision in the dispute. It seemed to be an impossible task; the two babies had looked much alike and nobody except the two mothers had skill to discern which was the mother of the living baby and which the dead. It was therefore the judges' opinion that Solomon himself should decide which woman lied and which spoke the truth.

Led before the king, each woman told her story, Agis, with a calm born of cunning, spoke well and seemed to convince many of the hearers, while Nipa, in her desperation, was wild in her accusation and almost incoherent, leaving most bystanders unimpressed by her case. Solomon listened intently, watching each woman's face as she spoke but saying nothing himself.

At length, the time came for the king to give his opinion. A silence fell on the court, broken only by Nipa's continued but suppressed weeping.

'In this unfortunate case,' pronounced the king, 'it is quite clear that one of you is lying and the other speaking the truth. What remains unclear is which is which. It is my opinion that because there are two of you, the chance of each of you lying is exactly half and half. I have therefore made up my mind and will proceed to judgement. Call in the executioner, and bring in the baby.'

A horrified silence fell as the court awaited the executioner's arrival. Solomon on his throne looked very stern and said nothing.

At last the executioner arrived, a huge masked man carrying a wickedly gleaming sword; he bowed low to the king and awaited his orders. Agis stood by defiantly holding the baby.

Finally Solomon spoke, 'Hear my judgement then,' he said. 'Because there is half a chance that each of you is this child's mother, you shall have half a child each. Lay the infant on the steps of my throne. Executioner, prepare to do your duty.'

Unhesitatingly, Agis laid the baby on the steps as Solomon commanded. Reluctantly, the executioner raised his sword. At once there was an ear piercing scream from Nipa as she flung herself forward and covered the baby with her own body, protecting it from the upraised sword's descent.

'No, my lord king,' she cried, 'give her the baby, spare its life. Punish me, spare the baby.'

Solomon raised his hand; the executioner, much relieved, stepped back. The king came down from his throne, raised Nipa to her feet and, with his own hands, placed the baby in her arms. 'You are the true mother,' he said, smiling, 'go home and look after your child.'

Then he turned to Agis, frowning. 'To you, I say, go in repentance, bury and grieve over your lost infant. Your doom is that everyone knows you for a liar, and worse. You laid down that baby to die; its real mother would have allowed you to brand her as the guilty one, would have gone under the sword herself, and would have done anything just so long as her child could live. Leave my sight at once and forever.'

13 King Solomon Source: The Bible

This is the famous story illustrating Solomon's insight and judgement in a tricky case. The choice of wisdom as the greatest gift is the key aspect of the early section; its application is seen in the second part. Maternal affection and jealousy are the twin points around which this part of the story is built.

- Solomon chose wisdom as the greatest gift, but what is wisdom?

- What might Solomon have chosen other than wisdom?

- Was Solomon's judgement cruel?

- Some mothers are competitive about their babies.
  Is this good for the babies?

- How should Solomon have dealt with the woman who lied?

14 Lady Godiva

How far would you go to help someone in need? Would you paint your nose bright red or shave off your eyebrows for charity? Would you really? How far would you go?

My story comes from the far-off times before William the Conqueror landed at Hastings and defeated the Saxon overlords of England.

It was a time when the country was settled under the rulership of its Saxon kings, and life went on in a fairly ordinary way, in most places at least. The rich feasted in their halls and the poor paid with taxes and labour in the fields. How happy you could be as a poorer person really depended on the character and values of the local overlord. If he was a fair and just ruler, then you were lucky; if he was a tyrant, then you were not. There was little that you could do to change the state of affairs in your corner of the kingdom.

Most people in the land were still workers on that land, ploughing, sowing and reaping crops for their overlord and growing a few strips of corn and vegetables for themselves, minding the pigs, milking the cows and shearing the sheep, living in village communities of a few families. There was a growing number of towns and cities, though, usually providing home, workshop space and a market for skilled trades such as silversmithing, shoemaking and weaving. The residents of these larger communities did not consider themselves to be as dependent on the overlord as did the village serfs, but they still depended on him for protection in times of unrest, and in return, they paid their taxes.

The city of Coventry was in Mercia, a wealthy province that may have been granted to Leofric in about 1013, making him one of the most powerful men in the land. He was certainly Earl of Mercia in the short reign of Harthacanute in 1040-42.

Harthacanute made himself deeply unpopular by imposing heavy taxation on the people. These taxes were so unpopular that angry mobs killed two of his tax collectors at Worcester. Harthacanute was so angry that he ordered his earls to burn the city and to destroy all the crops and livestock in the area. Worcester was the city of Leofric's own tribe, the Hwicce, so he must have found it very difficult to obey the king in this matter.

In Coventry, he and his young wife, Lady Godiva, famed for her beauty, earned a reputation as just and pious benefactors by founding a Benedictine monastery in 1043 to improve the education of the clergy. While Leofric became more involved with the finances of the growing town, and took over responsibility as its treasurer, Godiva built a reputation for her personal devotion to Mary, mother of Jesus, and for her interest in the arts, which she believed would improve the minds of the peasantry. The peasantry, however, had other things on its mind: survival, for one thing, and paying the heavy taxes for another.

What happened next is the stuff of legend. The story goes that Godiva became aware of the hardship suffered by the ordinary people and asked her husband, the treasurer after all, and a rich man, to excuse the population from paying their taxes that year.

Leofric refused. Godiva persisted in her request, and so it went on. At last, in an attempt to put Godiva off once and for all, Leofric declared that he would agree to excuse the common people their tax burden if, and only if, his lovely wife would ride naked through the city. After all, he pointed out, she was always trying to persuade the common people to take an interest in art, and what could be more artistic than the perfection of Godiva's lovely body? A deep blush spread over Godiva's face at the very thought of doing what her husband suggested. She was silent, and no doubt Leofric thought he had won his point and thought little more of the matter.

Godiva, however, could not let the matter stop there. Daily she was made aware of the desperate straits in which most of the population of Coventry lay, and at last she came to a daring decision. She would take Leofric at his word and ride naked through the city.

Anxiously, Godiva discussed with her ladies how such a shocking and daring thing could be done. One advised her to loosen her mass of golden hair and allow it to hang about her like a living curtain. Another suggested letting the townspeople know what she planned and asking them for their help in preserving her decency. It seemed like a big risk, but both plans were approved.

Like ripples in a pond, the word of Lady Godiva's ride spread through the community. Of course, there was some rude laughter and fun to be had from the idea, but when the purpose of the ride was explained, even the roughest of folk, struck by Godiva's bravery and generosity, vowed to stay indoors during the ride, shutters closed, so that she could pass by unseen.

At last the day came, and two of her ladies, fully clothed and armed like knights, brought Godiva's beautiful grey horse to the entrance of her apartments. Wrapped in a velvet cloak, Godiva came quickly down and mounted with the assistance of more of her ladies. There was no one else to be seen. Allowing the cloak to fall around her on the horse's back and shielded by her glorious hair, Godiva rode, eyes downcast, between her ladies, through the gateway and out into the cobbled streets of the city.

There was nothing to be heard in the normally busy highways and byways; all houses were closed and shuttered as though wrapped in a midday sleep. On and on rode the three ladies, hearing only the sound of their horses' hooves and the creaking of their harness. Not a soul was to be seen: the townspeople were keeping their promise. As Godiva passed under one window, she did hear a stifled gasp from behind the shutter, but that was all.

Leofric, meanwhile, had been at work among his papers all the morning and was unaware of what was happening. It was just as he finished his tasks and stood at the window to breathe in relaxing fresh air that Godiva entered the gates, returning from her ride. In disbelief, he watched as his wife's ladies hurried out to meet her, throwing the cloak once more about her lovely body and helping her to dismount and hurry back inside.

Long minutes passed as he stood there in astonishment, then gradually, as though at dawn, the castle began to come back to life. First the serving maids began to scurry on errands about the yard, followed cautiously by pages and menservants, while beyond the gates he could hear the sound of returning traffic as the city came back to life.

There came a soft knocking at the door, and a page announced the Lady Godiva. Leofric bid her enter, and Godiva, richly dressed as usual, entered and made a low curtsey. 'My lord,' she said, 'I have this day ridden naked through Coventry. Will you keep your word and remit the taxes of the citizenry?'

Leofric bade her be seated and asked her to tell him in detail what had happened. He was particularly impressed when he heard how loyally the people had supported his lady. 'Are you sure that no one saw you?' he asked.

'I think, perhaps, one person may have peeped from between their shutters in Broadgate, but that is all, I am quite sure,' she replied.

'In that case, what else can I do, my dear wife, than grant your wish? One exception I must make, however, and this will affect only the richer sort: I must keep the tax on riding horseback!'

The rejoicing in the city was great when the tax remission was announced. One person, however, did not share in the rejoicing. Earl Leofric had not forgotten about those shutters in Broadgate and made enquiries. What he discovered was that a young man called Tom has been unable to resist taking a crafty look through his shutters. Tom came under the earl's most severe displeasure, and furthermore, from that day on he had to put up with being called 'Peeping Tom' by the entire neighbourhood, signifying the disgust in which his behaviour was held by everyone in the community.

Now whether the story is true or not, or made up later by the monks to encourage pilgrims to the city, is not known. Certainly, Godiva lived and went down in real history for her beauty and piety. The golden wavy hair is probably true too, for just a few years ago, archaeologists discovered a shard of glass under the east window of the old cathedral which shows the face of a beautiful woman with a crown of golden wavy hair. It would be in this window that pictures of noble patrons would have appeared, so the place seems right too.

If you visit Coventry today, you will see a fine bronze statue of Lady Godiva in Broadgate, and if you wait for the clock to strike, you may catch a glimpse of Peeping Tom. Coventry, at any rate, has not forgotten Lady Godiva, and probably never will.

14 Lady Godiva Source: Traditional

Probably not true, this story features real historical benefactors of Coventry in the years before the Norman Conquest. It deals rather neatly with the dilemma many campaigners face of how far to become personally involved in a worthy cause.

- Are taxes fair?

- Do we judge people by what they wear?

- Leofric probably inherited his power over the people. Is inherited power still an issue today?

- Why is nudity embarrassing?

- Did Peeping Tom deserve his punishment?

15 Calandrino's Pig

Calandrino, Bruno and Buffalmacco were painters in fourteenth-century Florence. Buffalmacco had a reputation for being a practical joker, while Calandrino was well known for being a gullible soul who would believe all sorts of nonsense. It was therefore the case that Buffalmacco, aided and abetted by Bruno, frequently played jokes at Calandrino's expense. On one occasion the jokers managed to convince Calandrino that he was pregnant, on another that he could work magic. Calandrino seemed never to learn not to trust these two jokers.

It was almost Christmas and Calandrino's wife was in bed with a bad cold. She was not in the best of moods, because she was not going to be able to make her annual visit to her estate near Florence. The purpose of this annual visit was to collect a newly killed pig from which she would provide for the forthcoming 12 days of Christmas festivity. She realised that she would have to send Calandrino on this errand and could only hope that he would not make a pig's ear of it, as he so often did.

'Go and kill the pig, salt it carefully and bring it back here,' she said, 'and see you take good care of it. Mind you do not go out drinking with those worthless friends of yours, do you hear me?'

'Yes, my dear,' answered Calandrino mildly, 'fetch the booze and stay off the pig. No, I mean the other way round, don't I? Never mind, you can rely on me,' he added as he took his leave of her and set off on the journey.

As he crossed the river by the new bridge, who should he bump into but Buffalmacco and Bruno. 'Come and buy us a drink,' invited Buffalmacco, hiding a smile, 'it's your turn to pay, I think.' Calandrino was well known for accepting drinks from others but seemed never able to stay when it came to his turn to pay for a round of drinks.

'No, I can't stop,' replied Calandrino, 'I'm off to the country estate to kill and salt the pig for Christmas, and the wife will kill me if I waste any time. Sorry, I've got to go,' and off he went up the hill.

Buffalmacco turned to Bruno. 'I think we should pay a visit to this pig,' he remarked, 'what do you think?'

'I'm on,' confirmed Bruno, so they too set off for the countryside in Calandrino's wake.

When Calandrino reached his wife's estate, he lost no time killing the pig and putting it ready to salt the next day. He was just sitting by the well with a jug of best Vernaccia wine when who should enter the courtyard but Bruno and Buffalmacco. 'Just in time for a drink, are we?' asked Bruno.

'There's only a drop left,' replied Calandrino, 'but I suppose I can let you have some.' and sending for some glasses, poured each of his guests a very small measure of wine, which they drank off cheerfully.

'You must come out for a drink with us tonight,' insisted Buffalmacco, our treat. Your wife will be none the wiser back in Florence. Now, where's that pig?'

Proudly, Calandrino took them to look at his handiwork, praising himself for his excellent management in growing so portly a porker and outlining his plans for salting it down the next day.'You surely are not going to waste that good pig on a lot of hungry relatives at Christmas,' exclaimed Bruno, 'sell it and let's have a good booze-up with the money. You can always tell your wife the pig was stolen.'

'Not a chance,' replied Calandrino, 'she would never believe me, and my life would not be worth living. Forget it. I suppose you're too busy to stay for supper, so maybe I'll see you later.' With that he hurried back into the house, leaving his two friends standing in the courtyard.

'We'll have that pig tonight,' remarked Bruno, 'it will be easy as long as he doesn't put it somewhere else before he comes out.'

Later in the evening, Calandrino remembered that he had been promised a drink by Buffalmacco, and unable to resist a free glass of wine, or three, set out for the tavern.

According to plan, Buffalmacco and Bruno kept Calandrino's glass so well filled without asking him to pay that he had become extremely merry by closing time. Heading home on unsteady feet, Calandrino opened the door and fell flat on his face on the kitchen floor, where he lay until morning, sleeping like a baby.

A while later, Bruno and Buffalmacco arrived, expecting to have to break in, but finding Calandrino snoring loudly with his feet sticking out of the doorway, they tiptoed gently past and made their escape, carrying the pig between them. They left the porker in the barn behind the priest's house where they were staying, and went off to bed.

Next morning, Calandrino woke up with a dreadful headache and no pig. He came into the village making a terrible outcry, and asking everyone he met whether they knew who had stolen his pig. It was pretty evident that he suspected everyone he met.

Eventually he reached the priest's house and met Bruno and Buffalmacco in the lane. 'Gone!' he cried. 'Somebody's pinched my pig! Nicked it,' he added loudly,' somebody round here!'

'I should shout a bit louder if I were you,' remarked Bruno, folding his arms and looking sternly at Calandrino,' we might even believe you if you do.'

'Believe me? What do you mean?' asked Calandrino, amazed.

'Well, you said last night you were going to sell it and party with the money. We both heard you, didn't we, Buffalmacco?'

'Yep,' agreed Buffalmacco, 'and what I want to know is, where is our share of the wine?'

'It was you that said that not me!' protested Calandrino, 'Oh, the wife'll kill me if I don't find that pig! Folks round here would nick anything. How am I going to find out who done it?'

' Well, if it wasn't you, then you'll have to ask all the blokes who were in the tavern last night; and if you say you can't trust anyone round here, then what you need is a lie detector, mate,' observed Bruno.

'Yes, lie detector,' gabbled Calandrino, 'who do we know who can detect lies?'

'Well, as a matter of fact, I can,' said Buffalmacco, 'given the traditional bread and cheese tablets, that is. Look, you lay on a few flagons of Vernaccia up at the estate and I'll get some bread and cheese tablets made up in Florence. A florin or two should cover the cost. It's a well-known fact that liars can't swallow bread and cheese.'

'Thanks, mate,' said Calandrino, handing over the money, 'I'll see you back there at, say, two o'clock. I'll need to round up all the fellows from the tavern, so I had better get on with it,' and off he went.

Buffalmacco and Bruno hurried off to the apothecary in Florence, where they had a set of sugar-coated pills made from bread, and two apparently identical pills made from Aloe Vera and Dog Ginger; these last two were secretly marked to distinguish them from the bread pills.

At two o'clock everyone met at the estate. Calandrino made a long speech in support of his lost pig and explained that everyone could prove their innocence by simply swallowing one of Buffalmacco's truth pills.

Solemnly everyone lined up and Buffalmacco walked along the line placing a sugared pill on each person's tongue. Bruno followed, filling a generous tankard of wine for each man. Of course, most of the men guessed that there was a joke afoot so everyone acted very solemnly, and enjoyed their wine as they waited for events to unfold.

When Buffalmacco got to Calandrino, he popped a marked pill into his victim's mouth. It tasted so vile that Calandrino spat it out at once. Buffalmacco pretended not to notice, but when Bruno arrived with the wine he cried out that the pill had not been swallowed. 'You must be the liar, Calandrino,' he cried, 'look at this pill in the dust!'

'Now, let's be fair,' said Buffalmacco, returning, 'It could have been a mistake, let's try another one to be sure,' and he pushed the second marked pill between Calandrino's lips.

Red in the face and with streaming eyes from the effort of keeping the foul and fiery pill in his mouth, Calandrino once more spat it out. Buffalmacco and Bruno looked very solemn. 'You must be the liar after all, you know. It's a bit much accusing all these good blokes like that. You'd better give them another drink to make amends, before they get annoyed, if you see what I mean.'

Dejectedly, Calandrino ordered fresh wine for everyone and went off to sit by the well, where he hoped to wash away the terrible taste of the pills. Pretty soon Bruno and Buffalmacco came up, wine in hand, 'You should have told the truth, mate,' Bruno observed.

'I don't know how we are going to tell your wife about this,' added Buffalmacco, sighing.

'My wife! Do not tell my wife about this!' cried Calandrino, 'I'd give a couple of Christmas capons for her not to hear about this!'

'Done!' cried Bruno, 'I could just fancy a nice juicy capon for Christmas dinner.'

'Me too,' agreed Buffalmacco, 'it would be worth keeping quiet for a capon. You can trust us, mate, we won't say a word.'

15 Calandrino's Pig
Source: The Decameron

This is a great story but could be offensive to some Muslim students, so use with care. Trickery, selfishness, and cruel 'humour' all come into the frame here.

- Is Calandrino being bullied?

- What does Calandrino need to learn about getting on with others?

- We may laugh at this story, but should we?

- Are practical jokes OK?

- Did Calandrino deserve to be tricked?

16 Orpheus and Eurydice

It is said that Orpheus, born of the sun god Apollo and the muse Calliope, was the greatest musician the world had ever known, or would ever know. He played the lyre, and such was his skill that when he sat on mountainside or in vineyard or olive grove and plucked its strings and allowed the music to flow, Nature itself stopped to listen. Lion and bear, wolf and deer, goat and sheep, all would come close to hear him, forgetting enmity and fear alike. The naiads, spirits of the trees, and dryads, spirits of the water, would come from woodland and stream to dance to the wonderful sound of his music.

On one such occasion, Eurydice, a wood nymph, enchanted by the music that she heard in her woodland clearing, stepped out to join the dance. She was fair and fairylike and seemed to float over the grass, so graceful were her steps. Her eyes sparkled with the excitement of the dance and her smile was enchanting.

It chanced that Orpheus, looking up from his lyre, saw Eurydice weaving through the dance, and her beauty held him amazed. For the first time in his life, his fingers faltered on the strings and his music fell silent. The dance ceased abruptly and all looked towards Orpheus to discover the reason for the lull the in music. So it was that Eurydice looked at Orpheus, to find that he was looking at her, and only her. Grey eyes gazed into brown across the clearing and in that moment soul reached out to soul and found true love.

Recollecting that a dance was in progress, Orpheus again struck his lyre, and the music recommenced; but the tune had changed. Such a hymn to love flowed from the instrument that many dancers wept for joy, and embraced each other for the happiness of living. Eurydice did not dance; as though pulled by a magnet, she walked gracefully through the dancers, coming nearer to Orpheus, never moving her eyes from his handsome face. At last she stood before him and, reaching out, simply touched his hand on the strings of the lyre. Orpheus put down the instrument and, standing, took the hand she offered. From that moment they were never apart.

A great feast was held and the god of marriage, Hymnaeios himself, blessed the couple. Everyone present rejoiced in their evident happiness and the celebrations went on far into the night. There was one person, however, who was not present at the wedding and who did not rejoice in their happiness: Aristaeus the shepherd.

Long before Eurydice set eyes on Orpheus, Aristaeus had seen her and desired to make her his own. Eurydice, however, had distrusted the wicked look in the shepherd's eyes and refused his gifts and invitations. Now that Eurydice had married Orpheus he was in a dark and dangerous mood of anger and bitter jealousy.

Aristaeus had decided that he would kill Orpheus and steal Eurydice away as they made their way home from the feasting. So there he waited near the dark pathway, waiting with wickedness in his heart. Soon Orpheus and his bride came, arms wrapped around each other, along the path, talking contentedly together, planning the happy future they would make.

Out leaped Aristaeus, dagger in hand. Orpheus was unarmed so immediately he grabbed Eurydice by the hand and together they fled though the forest, closely followed by Aristaeus. The chase was long and desperate, but just as Orpheus thought they were getting away, Eurydice shrieked and fell to the ground. Orpheus turned to face Aristaeus, unarmed as he was, but Aristaeus gave a harsh laugh and pointed to where Eurydice lay, then he shrugged and walked off the way he had come.

Turning back to Eurydice, Orpheus found her still and silent, pale as death. Tiny trickles of blood ran from her heel and told Orpheus her fate. In their flight, Eurydice had stepped unaware into a nest of vipers and they had bitten deadly poison deep into her heel. There was no hope, Orpheus realised, none at all. Orpheus cradled Eurydice tenderly as a baby as the last faint breath left her body and her soul fled weeping to the underworld kingdom of Hades, god of the shades of the dead.

Orpheus was inconsolable, he wept through the long days and weeks that followed and nothing could bring light or hope into his life at all. At last, he strapped his lyre to his back and set off to see if he could find his way into the Underworld, to beg Hades to have mercy and restore Eurydice to life.

The journey was long and dark with terrible obstacles to overcome, but Orpheus used his gift of music to avert danger and destruction and at last came to the gates of the Underworld, a deep primeval cavern, guarded by the great three-headed dog Cerberus. Even Cerberus was melted to pity by the sadness in the music that Orpheus then played, and allowed him to pass through the gates, downward, always downward, until at last he reached the throne where Hades sat with his wife Persephone.

The Lord and Lady of the Underworld listened to Orpheus' song of longing and love and loss; tears of sympathy ran down the lady's face and even the heart of her stern lord was touched with pity. Hades gave his judgement that he would allow Eurydice to return to life on one condition. Orpheus was to lead her out of the gates of Hades, but was on no account to look back at her until she had passed out into the light of day; if he did so, she would be taken back into the Underworld and there would be no second chance.

Gratefully, Orpheus accepted these conditions and, strapping his lyre to his back once more, began the steep climb back to the gates. The climb was long and hard; and behind him, Orpheus could hear Eurydice gasping for breath, so he slowed his pace to help her, longing but not daring to turn back and give her his assistance. A faint glimmer of light ahead told him that the gates were not far away, and he began again to quicken his pace, desperate to reach the light and hold his much-loved wife in his arms again.

Cerberus, on duty to prevent any soul's escape, lay still and watched him pass through every one of his three pairs of eyes. There was no warning growl from any of his three throats; Orpheus was safe to go. He stepped freely into the cool fresh air and light of the sun. Eurydice was still following, he was sure. Straining his ears, Orpheus could catch the sound of her laboured breathing as she made her way up the slope. He listened intently and with growing hope. Then there came a pause, a faint gasp of fear, as Eurydice approached Cerberus' lair, there by the gates to life. Orpheus heard with alarm a low rumbling growl rising from the guardian of the gates, and as he listened it grew to a snarl.

Without stopping to think, Orpheus sprang back into the tunnel, intending to protect Eurydice from attack. It was a terrible mistake: as their eyes met, the condition Hades had imposed was broken. Inexorably, Eurydice was dragged by an invisible force back down into the kingdom of the dead, never to return. The last Orpheus ever saw of her was the look of despair in her grey eyes as she was taken from him forever.

16 Orpheus and Eurydice
Source: Greek mythology

This traditional story of love and loss is an opportunity to explore issues of bereavement, framed in a way that may make it easier for group members.

- Would it ever have been possible to end this story happily?

- If Eurydice had lived, would their love have stayed the same or changed?

- The Greeks believed that spirits in the underworld endlessly longed to return to their lost life. Are our beliefs any more comforting?

- Can 'love at first sight' really exist?

- In what ways do people respond emotionally to music?
  Why do some of us do so?

17 Rescue in the Southern Ocean

There is a yacht race that uniquely tests sailors' skill and strength and personal courage. It is called the Vendée Globe, because once every four years, a small fleet of about 20 boats sets off from Les Sables d'Olonne in the Vendée region of western France. The competitors sail due south towards Antarctica, then turn eastwards round the Cape of Good Hope to circle the southern hemisphere at about 40 degrees latitude, in seas that are famed for their storms and fearsomely high waves. They do all this in boats of about 70 feet in length; and they do it alone, for this is a race for lone sailors.

If a person enters the Vendée Globe, they must come to terms with the notion that, for much of the time, they will be far beyond the help of any emergency services or coastguards. They must be self-sufficient enough to cope with any repairs or emergencies that may arise in the boat and able to do without sleep for many hours at a time. They must survive polar cold in their wet, unheated cabins and maintain the focus and determination to guide their vessel safely through the four-month voyage.

Alone in the southern ocean, where waves can be higher than a house, the sailors appreciate the VHF radios and satellite communications with which each boat is provided. They can speak to race control, to other competitors, lost to sight in the vastness of the ocean, and to loved ones at home. They can video and transmit images of their experiences across the globe and feel a little bit less isolated than they really are.

Every competitor hopes that their luck will hold and that they will not suffer an accident or a serious injury so far from help. This is the story of when Frenchman Yann Elies, in his boat *Generali*, ran out of luck.

It was Thursday, 18th December 2008. There was a strong gale blowing and Yann Elies had set his sails and steering to cope with the bad conditions while he went forward to the bow of his vessel to carry out an essential repair. He was wearing his lifejacket and his harness was attached to the boat, so while the move forward was unpleasant and challenging, it was relatively safe.

The waves were high and coming at the boat from awkward angles, but there was nothing he could do about that, so he was making the best of a bad job. It was while he was working at the bow that the yacht ran slap into a huge wave. It was like hitting concrete, and the yacht stopped in its track, flinging Yann violently against the railing, and passed by leaving him in agony.

Yann was pretty certain that his thigh was broken, and his ribs hurt, too. In that moment, his race was at an end and his fight for survival began; first of all with a desperate struggle to reach the relative safety of his cabin. It was searingly painful, dragging himself back along the side decks, into the cockpit and finally into his bunk, and by the time he got there, he was finished. He would be able to move no more.

The VHF was just in reach, so Yann was able to radio race control, report the disaster that had overtaken him and talk with the race doctor, who confirmed that he had probably broken his femur. All competitors carry powerful painkillers such as morphine. Yann was instructed to take some at once, and meanwhile a rescue attempt would be started. The only problem was that Yann, only six feet away from the vital first aid box, was in too much pain to reach either it, or his food or water.

The accident occurred in one of the loneliest areas of the globe, 800 miles south of Australia, and far beyond the reach of anything like a rescue helicopter. The Australian Navy was asked for its help and immediately set about providing assistance. There was a medically equipped frigate called the *Arunta* in harbour at Freemantle, Perth, and this was readied and despatched by about 1800 on the evening of the accident, Thursday. At best, given the bad weather, *Arunta* was not expected to be able to reach *Generali* before Sunday evening at the earliest, so Yann was in for a dangerous and lonely time. The shock of the injury, dehydration or a blood clot could easily kill him; more needed to be done.

In previous situations of this kind, the value of another human soul being nearby had been identified as a key factor in the victim's survival. Race organisers therefore ordered the two competitors nearest *Generali* to abandon their race and head to Yann's position in order to offer him support. In spite of Yann's desperate situation, both Marc Guillemot and Sam Davies were forbidden to attempt to board *Generali* because conditions were so dangerous. Such an action could only be allowed if Yann was about to die. Both Marc and Sam made for Yann's position as quickly as they could, all thoughts of the race becoming secondary to the need to offer whatever help they could.

Sam Davies, racing 300 miles to get to the scene aboard her yacht Roxy, said, 'I'm ready to do anything I can to help, as I am sure any of the other skippers in this race would be. The trouble is, as Yann cannot move and we are alone on our boats in quite big seas, there is little we can do other than offer company and moral support as we await the rescue.'

Marc Guillemot on *Safran* was fortunate in being much nearer to *Generali* when the accident occurred and by 0615 the next morning, Friday, he was within a mile of his good friend Yann. Marc understood what Yann was going through because, some three years earlier, he had suffered two broken legs during a solo race and had had to endure three agonising days waiting for rescue. He offered advice and support to his friend over the radio and, by repeatedly sailing across the stern of *Generali*, tried to throw in some packets he had prepared, containing water and morphine tablets. The seas were too rough and the attempt failed, but Yann knew that his friend was close by and would not abandon him.

Later in the day, Marc pushed him to try again to reach some painkillers. Yann could not reach the medical box but was able to get to some paracetamol and a can of condensed milk. It was not much, but it was a help and, when the paracetamol took effect, he was able to then reach the morphine and water. Thus, more comfortable and knowing that he was no longer alone, Yann was able to get some sleep overnight.

Next day, Saturday, brought a most welcome sight. The Australian Navy had worked wonders and an emotional Marc Guillemot broadcast news of the arrival of *Arunta*. He said afterwards that his eyes may have been playing tricks, but that he thought it came in escorted by a crowd of joyful, leaping dolphins.

The *Arunta* immediately took up station broadside on to *Generali*, acting as a wave break and creating calm water for the rescue. A Zodiac inflatable boat came out from the frigate and lost no time in putting an experienced sailor on board *Generali*, who then made it safe for two medics to climb aboard. While these officers went in to prepare Yann for transfer, the Zodiac crossed to where an emotional Marc was filming the rescue. They had brought him a few presents, an ANZC beanie hat, a bottle of wine and some cheese; 'and I don't have a corkscrew aboard,' lamented Marc later.

It took just 20 minutes from the arrival of *Arunta* for the Australian Navy to have Yann tucked up in the radio officer's cabin, receiving expert medical help.

Marc and Sam, much relieved at the success of the rescue, were given permission to continue their race, which they did successfully by mid-February, Marc coming third and Sam coming fourth. Needless to say, Yann was there on the quayside to welcome them home.

As for *Generali*, it sailed away under automatic pilot to be lost in the vastness of the southern ocean.

17 Rescue in the Southern Ocean
Source: Vendée Globe 2008-09 newsfeeds

This is a true account of a life-and-death situation which developed during the 2008-09 Vendée Globe yacht race. It invites questions concerning the justifications and costs associated with risk taking.

- Why should people be allowed to take part in activities that can, and do, claim lives?

- The Australian Navy had no hesitation in going to the rescue. Was it worth the huge expense?

- Why did the arrival of Marc Guillemot make such a difference to Yann when he knew there was no chance of Marc coming on board to help him?

- Sam knew there was very little chance of reaching Yann before the Navy, but she still tried her hardest to get there. Why?

- Why do people risk their lives to help others?

18 Miracle Landing

The word 'miracle' is usually taken to refer to a wonderful happening that cannot be explained by ordinary means. Whether the story I am about to tell you counts as a miracle, I will leave to you to decide.

The events of this day in New York are a matter of record. Headlines across the world carried the story; few people on the planet were unaware of the event. This is what happened.

We begin at La Guardia Airport, New York City, on a cold day in January 2009. Flight 1549 with 155 passengers aboard is waiting for permission to take off. Captain Chesley B. Sullenberger III ('Sully') is in command of this routine journey to Charlottesville, South Carolina. At 58, Sully is a veteran pilot; he served as a fighter pilot in the US Air Force through most of the 1970s and has 29 years' service with US Airways as a civil aviation pilot. He is an expert on air safety. Sully's co-pilot is at the controls for the take-off, and as they get clearance from air traffic control, the noise of the twin engines rise to the familiar screaming pitch of take-off. Flight 1549 is on its way.

What is not apparent on the controller's radar is the flock of geese on collision course with the airbus at only 3,000 feet above the city. Less than a minute after take-off, the plane collides with the birds. 'You could hear them,' said Sully later, 'loud thumps. It felt like the airplane was being pelted with heavy rain or hail. It sounded like the worst thunderstorm I'd ever heard growing up in Texas.'

At this moment, both engines fail. The silence in the cockpit is shocking to the crew: where there should be power, there is none at all. The airbus has turned into a giant glider, with 155 people aboard, drifting above the densely packed streets and buildings of New York.

Sully takes control, 'My aircraft,' he says to his first officer, and receives the reply, 'Your aircraft'. Later he says that it has been the most sickening feeling he has ever experienced in his life, but that having been trained to remain calm, he now relies on that training. Certainly, the voice in which he reports the emergency to La Guardia shows no sign of panic.

At first it is hoped that the aircraft can stay aloft long enough to make a safe return to La Guardia, and runways are being cleared as the emergency procedures get under way.

'No,' Sully reports, the return to La Guardia is impossible. Controllers then alert a small airstrip on the other side of the Hudson River and orders it to prepare for a crash landing. They inform the pilot of this option. Shortly afterwards, again Sully radios, 'No'.

'You are not landing at Teterboro?'

'No, we are unable.'

'You are not landing at La Guardia?'

'No.'

'Where will you be landing?'

'The Hudson.'

'Say again, the Hudson?'

Radio silence as the plane dips below communication altitude.

The tower orders a tourist helicopter in the area to divert and keep relaying information about the fate of the aircraft.

Meanwhile, aboard the aircraft, the cabin is filled with the smell of burning and passengers realise that they are facing death. There is no panic aboard. Some passengers use their mobiles to leave messages for their loved ones, and later say that they felt a sense of peace from being able to say 'goodbye'. Jeff Kolodjay, travelling out for a fishing holiday with his son, has seen the engines on fire, and realises that the minor inconvenience of sitting apart from his son through a booking muddle has now turned into the possibility that they will each die alone.

In the cockpit, the co-pilot works through the procedure for trying to restart the engines, again and again without success, while Sully, at the helm, assesses the situation. The plane is too low to make La Guardia safely and, in his judgement, will crash into the skyscrapers of Manhattan if he risks the landing at Teterboro. There is only one place in New York wide enough and flat enough for him to land an airliner, and that is the icy cold Hudson River. It is here that Sully decides he must attempt a landing.

As 911 calls pour to the emergency services from shocked office workers, Sully makes his approach. Barring his way is the giant George Washington Bridge, crowded with traffic as usual. Taking his aircraft at a tilt across one end, Sully clears it with 200 feet to spare, then makes his final adjustment to line up with the river. He knows that the aircraft must be landed at a particular angle and speed; too fast, too slow, too shallow or too steep will result in disaster and, probably, death for everyone aboard. Sully also knows that the river is at freezing point and that survival in the water will depend on rapid rescue. His training tells him that he must ditch as near to shipping as possible. He must balance all factors and make the best of his options, and there is no time to waste.

Sully makes a passenger announcement, telling everyone to brace for impact. One person on the flight recalls that there was largely silence, broken only by the cabin crew saying steadily in unison, 'Brace, brace, brace, brace, brace, brace.' 'It was weird, like robots,' he recalls. Many pray.

The plane coasts in to land so smoothly that crew report later that they feel just a bump, and only then realise that they are in the river, as freezing cold water rushes in from the damaged tail section.

In the cockpit, Sully jokingly remarks to his co-pilot, 'Well, that wasn't as bad as I thought it would be,' then gives the one word command, 'evacuate'.

Passengers are ushered out on to the wings, slippery with aviation fuel and only inches above the ice floes of the Hudson River. Everyone co-operates in ensuring that women and children are the first to escape. Jeff Kolodjay recalls that Captain Sullenberger stood calmly in the gangway, courteously ushering his passengers out on to the wing. Only when he is quite sure that there is nobody left in the sinking aircraft, walking up and down the gangway twice to make certain, does Sully himself leave.

Captain Sullenberger has managed to put down his aircraft safely and as near as possible to the stretch of the Hudson where the ferry boat service crosses. Time is of the essence; and mercifully, the ferries begin arriving within minutes to pick up the survivors, some of whom are in the water. With his mind full of anxiety about the fate of his son, Jeff Kolodjay nevertheless enters the water to rescue a young woman who has slipped on the aviation fuel and fallen in the river. One wet survivor, pulled into a liferaft, is told by the pilot, 'You will die if you don't get those wet clothes off, sir.' Then, to the man's amazement, the pilot takes off his own shirt and gives it to him.

Ferry crews improvise ways of getting the cold survivors up the steep sides of their vessels and throw buoyancy aids to people waiting on the wings of the steadily sinking aircraft.

The NYPD scuba team is scrambled and hovers over the scene in its helicopter. Spotting a woman drowning in the water, and unable to come in any lower on the scene, divers risk their lives, jumping from 20 feet to rescue her. Then they enter the sinking aircraft to check for anyone trapped in the wreckage. There is no one, confirming what Captain Sullenberger calmly reports to rescue services: 'There is nobody left in that plane.'

Kindly police officers make every effort to locate Jeff Kolodjay's son, who is found safe and well, having been evacuated on to the wing opposite to that of his father.

Up and down the river, many New Yorkers have witnessed the landing and rescue operation. It is later said that the feeling of relief across the city, when it was known that everybody had survived, was tangible. To a city still scarred by the memory of the 911 twin towers disaster, this successful rescue seems to offer a kind of healing. Some survivors report that the experience has made them think again about what is most important in their lives. Everyone salutes Captain Sullenberger as the hero of flight 1549.

18 Miracle Landing
Source: Various newsfeeds 2009

Again, this is a true story, and one that made world news. Resourcefulness, courage, humour in the face of adversity and determination all come into play, but so too do considerations about the human spirit.

- Was this landing a miracle?

- If the pilot had not been flying fighter planes, would he have had the skills to deal with this emergency?

- Many messages came in to Captain Sullenberger after this event. One from a holocaust survivor said, 'If you save a life, you save the world.' What might this mean?

- Being able to say 'goodbye' was important to some people. Why might this be so?

- What is a hero?

19 The Real Robinson Crusoe

In 1720 Daniel Defoe published a novel that was to become one of the best-known books ever written. *Robinson Crusoe* has scarcely been out of print since, and has been translated into many languages across the globe. It is well known that Defoe based his story on the adventures of Alexander Selkirk, a real-life castaway.

Selkirk was a wild young man. Born in 1676, he grew up in Lower Largo in the Kingdom of Fife, the seventh son of a cobbler. Decent Scottish life in those days was sober and god-fearing; and the Presbyterian Church of Scotland, or Kirk, sternly controlled behaviour. In 1695, Selkirk was summoned before the Kirk Session following a violent family fight, caused by his brother trying to make him drink sea water. He did not bother to wait for the hearing, but ran away to sea.

In those days, the British government effectively encouraged piracy by issuing ships' commanders with 'letters of marque'. Such a letter entitled the bearer to sail the high seas, attacking and pillaging any ships they found belonging to nations with which Britain was at war, usually France and Spain. Vast fortunes could be made in this way and many a young man who was not too particular about right and wrong did what Selkirk did and joined these privateers. He did well and rose to the position of sailing master.

The privateering expedition that was to change his life was led by William Dampier and its purpose was to 'take, sink, burn or destroy' Spanish ships off the coast of South America, especially the annual treasure galleon. Selkirk was appointed sailing master on the 16-gun, 90-ton *Cinque Ports*. This expedition was a disaster. Captain Dampier, the leader, was deservedly unpopular, having just been court-martialled for cruelty to his Royal Navy crew and stripped of his Royal Navy status. This disgrace did not prevent him being given a letter of marque by Queen Anne, and in April 1703 Dampier set sail for the Pacific in the *St George* in company with the *Cinque Ports* with Selkirk aboard. Captain Thomas Straddling of the *Cinque Ports* appears to have been an even worse tyrant than Dampier himself, turning his ship into a kind of hell afloat.

The expedition was plagued by drunkenness and dissent, with members of the crews leaving the expedition whenever they got the chance. It was in September 1704 when they were amid the islands of the Juan Fernández grouping the south Pacific, that Selkirk found himself in violent disagreement with Straddling about the safety of the *Cinque*

Ports. As sailing master, it was Selkirk's opinion that, following a number of fights with the Spanish, the ship was in danger of sinking and needed to put in at the islands for urgent repairs. The captain dismissed his report and decided to carry on with the voyage regardless. Selkirk had no intention of going with him.

The islands were known to Dampier from an earlier voyage and he made no objection when Selkirk insisted upon being put ashore on the uninhabited island of Más a Tierra, where indeed, Dampier had found a marooned Mosquito Indian on his previous visit. There were goats, rats and cats on the island, left by previous voyagers, and Selkirk had with him a musket and some ammunition, some clothes, bedding and tobacco, and his Bible.

With these few supplies, Selkirk settled down to await rescue, reading his Bible to pass the time. He probably thought that he would have to wait for no more than a few weeks for a friendly vessel to pass, but it soon became clear to him that he was going to be on the island for much longer than he had expected and he began to make his island home more comfortable. He made clothes from goatskins and built two shelters from pimiento trees.

After a year or two he had a frightening and dangerous experience when two ships put in for water. Unthinkingly, Selkirk rushed to the shore but realised too late that the landing party were Spanish, They opened fire on him, forcing him to run for his life. The landing party hunted for him, but Selkirk knew his island better than they did and managed to hide up a tree until they gave up and left.

Meanwhile, Dampier's ship had returned to England alone because, as Selkirk had foretold, the *Cinque Ports* was unseaworthy, and had sunk with the loss of all hands except the captain and about six sailors. The Bristol merchants who had funded the venture were so dissatisfied that they decided to sue Dampier; and at the same time there was a war of words in the press between Dampier and disgruntled members of the expedition, which reflected very badly on his conduct of the voyage.

The lure of gold from the Spanish treasure galleons, however, proved as strong as ever and the Bristol consortium decided to fund another voyage. This time they equipped two ships, the *Duke* and the *Duchess*, and placed the expedition under the command of Captain Woodes Rogers who, incidentally, was a friend of Daniel Defoe. Whatever else Dampier may have been, he was a brilliant navigator, with achievements remembered to this day. Woodes Rogers asked the owners if he might take Dampier with him as navigator on the Duke; they agreed to drop the case against him and he set sail with Woodes Rogers on 1 August 1708.

The voyage proceeded, and by 2 February 1709 the two ships lay off the island of Más a Tierra. The landing party went ashore for water and to investigate the signal fire that somebody had lit on the island as they came into anchor.

The boat brought back crayfish in plenty and a wild-looking man, dressed in goatskins and hardly able to remember how to speak, not having done so for so long. Dampier informed the captain that the man was Selkirk and an able ship's master.

Edward Cooke, second in command on the *Duchess*, recounted that when Selkirk met the landing party and found that they were English, he was at first overjoyed. He then enquired whether Dampier was aboard the ships and, on being told that he was, changed his mind about being rescued and had to be strongly persuaded on board.

Selkirk had spent much time ashore in reading his Bible and in prayer, saying in later times that he was a better Christian on the island than at any other time in his life. He seemed quite unscathed by the experience and resumed his career as a privateer at once; within a year he was master of the ship that had rescued him.

Meanwhile, back in Largo, his family had long since given him up for dead; but in 1712, with a fortune of £800 in his pocket, he retired from the sea and returned home. It must have caused quite a stir in the small congregation as Selkirk entered the Kirk one Sunday, dressed in finery and unrecognisable to everyone except his mother.

Selkirk settled down to write his memoirs, which sold well when they came out in 1713, but the old wildness was still part of his make-up. He ran away to London with a local dairymaid, whom he then abandoned when he signed on to the Royal Navy on *HMS Weymouth*. Later, he married a Devon barmaid. At last, leaving two conflicting wills, each naming a different 'wife' as beneficiary, he sailed away to die of yellow fever in 1721 off the coast of West Africa.

19 The Real Robinson Crusoe

Source: *William Dampier, Buccaneer Explorer,* London, The Folio Society.

Gilchrist, J. (2009) Lost in the myth: the real Alexander Selkirk, *The Scotsman,* 27 January 2009

Fact and fiction collide here with interesting reflections on the age of exploration when people appear to have been left on islands fairly casually, and equally casually collected later.

- What is solitude?

- What if we had to do without the comforts of modern life.

- Was it weak or strong of Selkirk to consider staying on his island because he so disliked Dampier?

- Why do people try to go to places no one else has been to?

- Selkirk– hero or villain?

20 Marco Polo

It is very hard when people do not believe what you say. Through the centuries, explorers have come back from their adventures to be met with covert or open disbelief. Such an early traveller was Marco Polo.

Polo was born in Venice in September 1254 and was the son of a wealthy trader, Niccolo. The family was making money by trading with the powerful Mongol Empire, which at that time extended well into Eastern Europe.

In 1264, Niccolò and his brother Maffeo joined a diplomatic mission sent by Ilkhan Hulagu Khan to his powerful brother, the legendary Kublai Khan, who had his capital in Beijing, then called Kanbaliq or Dadu. Kublai Kahn was friendly towards the Polos and interested in their culture and religion. He sent them back to the Pope with a letter asking the Pope to send educated persons who could instruct his court and people in Christianity. As an aid to travel, the letter was accompanied by a golden tablet a foot long, which acted as the Khan's command that the travellers be given food and horses all along the route while they were within his kingdom.

The Pope sent just two missionaries with the Polos, who began their return journey in 1271. Marco, aged 17 was able to join the expedition to Cathay (China). The two monks left the expedition on the route, because they were afraid of what might be at the journey's end, but the Polos carried on and reached Kanbaliq in 1274, handing presents from the Pope to the Khan.

It seems that the Khan was not angry at the relative failure of the Polos' mission, for he kept them at court and appears to have been particularly friendly with Marco, whom he valued as a storyteller, and whom he sent on a number of diplomatic missions. These journeys gave Marco a unique opportunity to see the country and customs of t he people in the Khan's vast empire.

Seventeen years passed in the court of Kublai Khan, and, although they had asked for permission to return home, the Khan still kept them there. Marco became accustomed to the fabulous wealth and strange customs. It appears that the Khan even made Marco governor of Yangzhou for three years, where there was a small Italian community.

At last, in 1291, Kublai Khan gave the Polos permission to leave for home and they set off in the train of the Mongol princess Kökechin, who was going to be married to the Ilkhan of present-day Iran. They arrived home in Venice in 1295.

The Polos became an overnight success, with crowds of people coming to listen to the travellers' tales. These, however, were not much believed, because the world of distant Cathay was so very different from what the sophisticated Venetians knew of the world, through their wide network of trading links. There is a tradition that Marco and his father and uncle, irritated by their fellow Venetians' lack of belief in their accounts of Cathay, held a great feast. The three of them appeared in front of their richly clad guests dressed in the costumes of simple Chinese peasants. As the banquet commenced they opened their costumes to show a vast fortune in precious stones in the pockets and sewn into the seams. It caused a sensation, but they were still not much believed.

Shortly afterwards, Marco was captured during a sea battle with the Genoans, who held him prisoner for three years. During this time, he shared a cell with Rusticello da Pisa, who wrote an account of Marco's journeys in unknown China. It was very popular and was translated into a number of languages, but because it was before the time of the printing press, many small points of difference crept into the text, adding to doubts about its truthfulness. Later, Marco published his own version, but this just added to the confusion.

Marco Polo died at home in January 1324, a wealthy man, leaving a wife and three daughters who all married into noble families.

The doubt about Marco Polo's account of his travels persists to this day, but there is no doubt that his writings inspired travellers and explorers then, and have done so ever since. One of these was Christopher Columbus, a native of Genoa where Polo was imprisoned, who set off in search of a western route to the East with its wealth of silks and spices, and discovered America instead.

Some of the passages in The Travels of Marco Polo do seem a bit far-fetched, as you may like to judge from these two extracts.

> In this province live huge snakes and serpents of such a size that no one could help being amazed even to hear of them. They are loathsome creatures to behold. Let me tell you just how big they are. You may take it for a fact that there are some of them ten paces in length that are as thick as a stout cask: for their girth runs to about ten palms. These are the biggest. They have two squat legs in front near the head, which have no feet but simply three claws, two small and one bigger, like the claws of a falcon or lion. They have enormous heads and eyes so bulging that they are bigger than loaves. Their mouth is big enough to swallow a man at one gulp. Their teeth are huge.

All in all, these monsters are of such inordinate bulk and ferocity that there is neither man nor beast but goes in fear of them. There are also smaller ones, not exceeding eight paces in length or six or it may be five.

You must know that by day they remain underground because of the great heat; at night they sally out to hunt and feed and seize whatever prey they can come by. They go down to drink at streams and lakes and springs. They are so heavy and of such a girth that when they pass through sand on their nightly search for food or drink they scoop out a furrow through the sand that looks as if a butt full of wine had been rolled that way.

Another thing about these serpents; they go to the dens where lions and bears and other beasts of prey have their cubs and gobble them up – parent as well as young – if they can get at them.'

We shall tell you next of *the experiment that is made, before embarking on a voyage, to find out whether the venture will fare well or badly. The seamen will take a hurdle–that is, a frame of wickerwork– and to every corner and side of it they will attach a rope, so that there are eight ropes in all, and fasten all the ropes together at the end of a long cable. Next, they will find some fool, or someone who is drunk for no one in his right sense would expose himself to so much risk, and lash him to the hurdle. This they do when it is blowing a gale. Then they set the hurdle upright in the teeth of the wind and the wind lifts it and carries it aloft, while the men hold it by hanging on to the cable. If the hurdle should tilt over while it is up in the air facing the wind, they give a slight tug to the cable and the hurdle returns to an upright position. Then they pay out more cable and the hurdle climbs higher. And so they continue, alternately tugging and paying out as the hurdle tilts and straightens till it would have climbed completely out of sight if only the cable were long enough. The point of the experiment is this. If the hurdle climbs straight up aloft, then it is said that the ship on whose behalf the experiment is conducted will make a speedy and profitable voyage, and all the merchants flock to her to pay freight and passage money. If the hurdle fails to rise, no merchant will enter this particular ship, because they say that she could not complete her voyage and all sorts of disasters would overtake* her. So this ship stays in port for that year.

Before dismissing either or both of these stories; consider that crocodiles are native to the region which Marco Polo was visiting when he claims to have witnessed these fabulous 'serpents'. With regard to the second fragment, the Chinese were known to have developed the skill of kite flying; and consider too that para-ascending, where a willing participant is towed into the air wearing an inflated parachute, is a popular sport in some seaside resorts today.

20 Marco Polo
Source: *the Travels of Marco Polo,* (1968)
Trans Latham, R, London, The Folio Society

The sojourn of the Polos in China was a catalyst for the increased travel a nd trade of succeeding generations. Much of what is in the *Travels* seems a bit exaggerated, but there is enough truth in them, together with external snippets of evidence, to make most scholars believe that the Polos did make the journey as described.

- Is seeing believing?

- Do we reject the unknown? If so, why?

- The story *could* have been a fake, but why would a wealthy, successful family want to lie?

- What is conspiracy theory? Is it unhealthy?

- Why was Kublai Khan interested in Western religion?

21 Socrates

If you ask people which philosophers they have heard of, the chances are that they will say 'Socrates'. So who was Socrates, and what was he like?

Socrates was a citizen of ancient Athens and was born in about 469 BC. His father, Sophroniscus, seems to have been a sculptor or stonemason and his mother, Phenarete, a midwife. Socrates probably followed his father into the trade, and traditionally, a sculpture of the three graces on the Acropolis is said to be his work.

All Athenian men had to do military service, and Socrates served as a hoplite, one of the heavily armed infantrymen who bought their own armour and had to be reasonably well-off to join. He fought in several campaigns, but found time to study too.

Socrates began by studying the sciences but became less and less interested in how things happened and worked in the world, and more and more interested in why things were as they were. Socrates asked himself and others many questions, most of which took a lot of discussion. There were no easy answers to the kinds of questions he asked, but Socrates was really more interested in exploring the questions themselves. It seems that he was getting a reputation for being very wise, and a result of this reputation, in about 421 BC, when he was 48, had a lasting effect on his life.

There was a cave at Delphi, the place where the god Apollo was believed to answer questions through the priestess serving there. A man called Chaerephon came to the Oracle at Delphi and asked if there was any person in Greece who was wiser than Socrates. The answer was that there was nobody wiser. The news of this reached Socrates and really disturbed him, for it seemed to him that the one thing he knew for sure was that he did not know very much: so few of his questions actually had answers.

Socrates became convinced that the sacred oracle had made a mistake and, because he believed that truth was very important, he set himself the task of finding somebody wiser than himself. He set about it by visiting all the people of his day who claimed to be very wise, and asking them some of the questions that he was puzzling over. One by one, these people failed to show that they were wiser than Socrates, the man who had thought of the questions in the first place. Some of them, of course, were claiming to be wise when they were not really so at all, in order to impress people; and Socrates had no hesitation in exposing fakes. Reluctantly, Socrates accepted that the oracle may have been right, because he realised that actually, everyone knew nothing; but he was wiser because he knew that he knew nothing, and the others did not.

Socrates had set out to challenge the fake 'wisdom' that seemed to be so impressive and next took to sitting in all the public places where people gathered, ready and available to discuss questions with anyone who wished to do so. Quite a number of the younger men of Athens gathered around him daily to hear and discuss. In this way, Socrates became a bit of a celebrity, very well known indeed. Unfortunately, all this discussion was keeping him from his work as a stonemason and not earning him any money. As the years passed, he became poorer and poorer, relying on handouts from the people who came to join his debates.

These debates will have covered questions such as 'what is courage?', and might have moved from examples of courage to an attempt to say what courage is in a general way, to find a definition that fits all examples. Sometimes a series of simpler questions would be used to get at the answer to a more complex one. The Greeks called this last method 'induction'.

Often the government of Athens will have been the subject of heated public debate: heady and dangerous stuff. The public questions he asked powerful members of the Athenian state often resulted in these men being made to feel foolish and humiliated, for Socrates had no idea of letting people off the hook of his sharp, intelligent, often humorous enquiries. Some of these people, especially Amytus, became his enemies and plotted to get rid of him.

First, Amytus persuaded Aristophanes to write a play ridiculing Socrates. It proved to be very popular, with even the potters cashing in on its popularity by making souvenir jugs with Socrates' face on them. Socrates, however, was untroubled and went to the theatre himself. When the play began he stood up where everyone could see him and, standing, watched the play quite happily.

Next, Amytus, Lycon and Meletus brought a prosecution against Socrates in the courts. The charges were that he did not believe in the gods worshipped by the city and introduced beliefs of his own; also that he corrupted the youth of the city with his ideas.

Lysias was appointed to defend him against the charges and showed Socrates the speech that he had prepared. This Socrates rejected because, he said, it was a good speech that made him sound like a lawyer, not a philosopher, and so would not suit him. His young follower Plato went up on the platform to speak in Socrates' defence but was shouted down because he was young. It therefore seems that Socrates was not defended at his trial, the outcome of which was that he was condemned by 281 votes to 275 against condemnation.

When the judges were considering what the sentence should be, Socrates suggested that he should be fined, but the judges were not happy with this suggestion. Socrates then gave it as his opinion that he should be given free meals for the rest of his life in recognition of what he had done for the state. This suggestion went down so badly that the judges condemned him to death by drinking hemlock and sent him to prison to await his end.

His friends bribed the guards and arranged an escape, but Socrates refused the opportunity to escape from prison because he said that he did not fear death, and that having consented to live under Athenian law, he should not break it by running from its judgement. He also made the point that he would really be no better off if he were to go elsewhere, because he would certainly fall foul of their authorities too, by continuing his questioning.

So, Socrates drank the hemlock and died, reminding his friend that he owed a sacrifice to the god of healing and asking him to see that it was done: 'Crito, we owe a cock to Asclepius. Please, don't forget to pay the debt.'

21 Socrates
Source: Ferguson, J. (ed.)
(1970) *Socrates: A Source Book,*
London, Macmillan.

Socrates himself left no writings, but was a profound influence on his followers, who did leave accounts. These accounts vary according to the interests of the writer, but for all that, a picture of the historical personality emerges.

- Socrates was absolutely concerned with trying to arrive at the absolute truth. Is this possible?

- Why not have a go at this one! 'What is truth?'

- Why might Socrates be an uncomfortable person to have around?

- Was Socrates mad to refuse to escape?

- Is it better to be poor and doing what you want to do, or to make a living doing what you would prefer not to spend your time on?

Philosophy Through Storytelling

Philosophical Discussion Cards

Pictures are a very useful way to facilitate philosophical questions and this collection of images and question suggestions provide an ideal stimulus to provoke reflection and debate.

- Images include cartoon bomb, danger sign, cute puppy, moon landing and a footprint in the sand.

- Includes a comprehensive instruction booklet.

- Suitable for all ages from five to 95.

Introducing philosophical discussions to your group will challenge how participants think about themselves and each other, as well as the world around them.

25 cards, 127 x 90mm, Instruction booklet, Boxed
ISBN 978 0 86388 770 3

Order code 003-5668

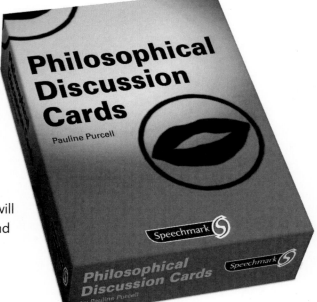

Philosophical Question Cards

These thought-provoking cards offer a selection of questions for philosophy sessions. The three categories are:

- What if... there are no computers

- Choices.
  Which would you choose... money or friends?

- What is... courage?

Suitable for all ages, from five to 95, these cards introduce philosophical scenarios for group discussion, which stimulate lively debate and elicit interesting opinions and perspectives from participants.
Using philosophy with your group offers the opportunity to develop thinking skills and will help group members to get to know each other.

52 cards, 127 x 90mm, Instruction booklet, Boxed
ISBN 978 0 86388 771 0

Order code 003-5667

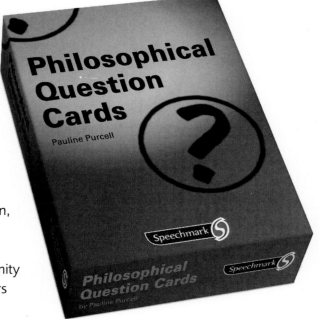